Microsoft

T0073658

Exam Ref DP-900
Microsoft Azure
Data Fundamentals

Second Edition

Nicola Farquharson

Exam Ref DP-900 Microsoft Azure Data Fundamentals
Second Edition

Published with the authorization of Microsoft Corporation by:
Pearson Education, Inc.

Copyright © 2024 by Pearson Education, Inc.

Hoboken, New Jersey

ISBN-13: 978-0-13-826190-0
ISBN-10: 0-13-826190-3

Library of Congress Control Number: 2024932734

1 2024

TRADEMARKS

WARNING AND DISCLAIMER

SPECIAL SALES

For information about buying this title in bulk quantities, or for special sales opportunities (which may include electronic versions; custom cover designs; and content particular to your business, training goals, marketing focus, or branding interests), please contact our corporate sales department at corpsales@pearsoned.com or (800) 382-3419.

For government sales inquiries, please contact governmentsales@pearsoned.com.

For questions about sales outside the U.S., please contact intlcs@pearson.com.

CREDITS

EDITOR-IN-CHIEF
Brett Bartow

EXECUTIVE EDITOR
Loretta Yates

ASSOCIATE EDITOR
Shourav Bose

DEVELOPMENT EDITOR
Songlin Qiu

MANAGING EDITOR
Sandra Schroeder

SENIOR PROJECT EDITOR
Tracey Croom

COPY EDITOR
Kim Wimpsett

INDEXER
Timothy Wright

PROOFREADER
Barbara Mack

TECHNICAL EDITOR
Owen Auger

EDITORIAL ASSISTANT
Cindy Teeters

COVER DESIGNER
Twist Creative, Seattle

COMPOSITOR
codeMantra

GRAPHICS
codeMantra

FIGURE CREDITS
Figure 4-13: Umamfals/ Shutterstock,
Figure 4-14: Ma8/123RF,
Figure 4-15: Yeliena Brovko/ Shutterstock

Contents at a glance

Contents

Introduction

Many study resources for technical exams focus on detailed, low-level tasks, teaching how to use specific functionalities and accomplish granular objectives. However, the DP-900 exam, which covers Microsoft Azure data fundamentals, adopts a more high-level approach. This exam is designed to build upon your basic understanding of data concepts and extend it to strategic application within Microsoft Azure's data services. It emphasizes a broad understanding of data management, storage, and processing in the Azure cloud environment. The DP-900 exam, and the materials aligned with it, are geared more towards conceptual understanding rather than intricate coding. Most of the code samples and discussions in this context aim to illustrate broader data principles and cloud data service applications, highlighting the strategic aspect of data handling in Azure rather than focusing on detailed coding techniques.

Ideal candidates include those at the outset of their data-related career path, IT professionals seeking to broaden their expertise into cloud data services, and academicians involved in teaching or learning data and cloud technologies. Even professionals from non-technical backgrounds will find the DP-900 exam valuable for understanding data management in the cloud context.

As for the required knowledge and experience, the DP-900 exam is tailored for individuals with a basic understanding of data concepts, including the creation, storage, and processing of data. It expects familiarity with both relational and non-relational data types, as well as an introductory knowledge of data analytics and reporting concepts. A general grasp of cloud concepts, especially around Microsoft Azure, is beneficial, though extensive prior experience is not necessary. The exam content covers Azure data services, data processing, and data storage solutions, so even a fundamental level of exposure to these areas can be advantageous for aspirants.

This book covers every major topic area on the exam, but it does not cover every exam question. Only the Microsoft exam team has access to the exam questions, and Microsoft regularly adds new questions to the exam, making it impossible to cover specific questions. You should consider this book a supplement to your relevant real-world experience and other study materials. If you encounter a topic in this book you are not completely comfortable with, use the "Need more review?" links in the text to find more information and take the time to research and study the topic. Great information is available on MSDN, on TechNet, and in blogs and forums.

Organization of this book

This book is organized by the "Skills measured" list published for the exam. The "Skills measured" list is available for each exam on the Microsoft Learn website: *Microsoft.com/learn*.

Each chapter in this book corresponds to a major topic area in the list, and the technical tasks in each topic area determine a chapter's organization. If an exam covers six major topic areas, for example, the book will contain six chapters.

Microsoft certifications

Microsoft certifications distinguish you by proving your command of a broad set of skills and experience with current Microsoft products and technologies. The exams and corresponding certifications are developed to validate your mastery of critical competencies as you design and develop, or implement and support, solutions with Microsoft products and technologies both on-premises and in the cloud. Certification brings a variety of benefits to the individual and to employers and organizations.

> **NEED MORE REVIEW?** **ALL MICROSOFT CERTIFICATIONS**
>
> For information about Microsoft certifications, including a full list of available certifications, go to *microsoft.com/learn*.

Check back often to see what is new!

Errata, updates, and book support

We've made every effort to ensure the accuracy of this book and its companion content. You can access updates to this book—in the form of a list of submitted errata and their related corrections—at *MicrosoftPressStore.com/ERDP9002e/errata*.

If you discover an error that is not already listed, please submit it to us at the same page.

For additional book support and information, visit *MicrosoftPressStore.com/Support*.

Please note that product support for Microsoft software and hardware is not offered through the previous addresses. For help with Microsoft software or hardware, go to *support.microsoft.com*.

Stay in touch

Let's keep the conversation going! We're on Twitter: *twitter.com/MicrosoftPress*.

About the author

NICOLA FARQUHARSON has more than two decades of experience in networking infrastructure and Microsoft technologies, such as artificial intelligence, Microsoft SQL, Microsoft Power BI, data science, Dynamics 365, machine learning, Microsoft Azure, and Azure DevOps. Her extensive background in these technologies ensures a deep and comprehensive coverage of the key concepts necessary for the Microsoft DP-900 certification exam.

Her career journey includes roles as a Microsoft technical trainer and professor, focusing on data, machine learning, and artificial intelligence. These roles have equipped Nicola with valuable insights into the skills and knowledge required in these rapidly advancing fields. Her experience as a cybersecurity/infrastructure senior analyst and IT consultant has also given her a profound understanding of data security and risk management, vital elements in contemporary data management.

Nicola's dedication to professional growth is reflected in her acquisition of multiple Microsoft technology certifications, including Microsoft AI Engineer, Microsoft Data Engineer, Microsoft DevOps Engineer Expert, Microsoft Teams Administrator Associate, Azure Security Engineer Associate, Microsoft 365 Enterprise Administrator, and Microsoft Cloud Solution Expert. These qualifications underscore her commitment to staying updated with the latest technological advancements. This second edition of *Exam Ref DP-900 Microsoft Azure Data Fundamentals* aims to provide readers with a thorough understanding of Azure data fundamentals, preparing them for the DP-900 exam and enhancing their career prospects in the fields of cloud and data technologies.

CHAPTER 1

Describe core data concept

Data has played an integral role in human endeavors throughout history, but its significance has surged exponentially in recent times, driven by technological advancements and the digital revolution. From ancient records inscribed on stone tablets to the vast digital repositories we have today, the evolution of data has profoundly shaped the trajectory of human progress. The field of data management and analytics has witnessed remarkable breakthroughs, fueled by the exponential growth of computing power and the escalating complexity of modern business challenges.

The structured organization of data originated during the emergence of relational databases in the 1970s. Visionaries like Edgar F. Codd revolutionized the field with their pioneering work on the relational model, laying the groundwork for structured data management systems so users can efficiently store, retrieve, and manipulate information. As technology advanced, the need to accommodate semi-structured and unstructured data formats became apparent. The explosive proliferation of the internet, social media, and Internet of Things (IoT) devices has given rise to novel data paradigms, spurring the development of specialized storage solutions and advanced analysis techniques.

In today's data-driven world, where knowledge is power, a firm grasp of the core concepts of data is imperative for individuals and businesses alike. This chapter embarks on a captivating journey, exploring the foundational principles of managing, storing, and utilizing data. By mastering these core data concepts, you will attain a solid understanding of how data is structured, stored, and processed within the dynamic Azure landscape. Prepare to explore the vast landscape of data to harness its transformative potential.

Skills covered in this chapter:

- Skill 1.1 Describe ways to represent data
- Skill 1.2 Identify options for data storage
- Skill 1.3 Describe common data workloads
- Skill 1.4 Identify roles and responsibilities for data workloads

Skill 1.1: Describe ways to represent data

In the world of data, the way information is structured and organized plays a crucial role in its effective management and utilization. There are three fundamental ways you can represent data: structured, semi-structured, and unstructured. Each representation offers unique characteristics and brings its own set of opportunities and challenges to the realm of data management.

By understanding these different ways to represent data, you and your organization can make informed decisions on how to store, process, and analyze your data effectively. Each data representation method offers distinct advantages and is suited to specific use cases. Whether it's the structured precision of relational databases, the flexibility of semi-structured data, or the untapped potential of unstructured data, embracing these representations empowers you to unlock the full value of your data assets.

This skill covers how to:

- Describe features of structured data
- Describe features of semi-structured data
- Describe features of unstructured data

Describe features of structured data

Structured data is a well-organized format that follows predefined schemas, providing efficient storage, retrieval, and analysis. It represents information in a tabular form with clear relationships between entities, making it highly suitable for relational databases. The structured nature of this data allows for easy sorting, searching, and querying using Structured Query Language (SQL). Examples of structured data include financial transaction records, customer profiles, and inventory management systems.

Imagine you have a structured data table representing sales transactions in a retail business. The table would have columns such as Transaction ID, Date, Customer Name, Product, Quality, and so on, as shown in Table 1-1. Each row would represent a specific sale, with corresponding values in each column. The structured format allows you and others in the business to efficiently track sales, analyze customer behavior, and generate insights for decision-making.

TABLE 1-1 Structured data

Transaction table						
Transaction ID	**Date**	**Customer Name**	**Product**	**Quality**	**Unit Price**	**Total Amount**
1	2023-05-10	John Smith	Smartphone	2	$500	$1,000
2	2023-05-11	Jane Doe	Laptop	1	$1200	$1,200
3	2023-05-11	Mark Johnson	Tablet	3	$300	$900

Structured data provides organizations with a consistent and organized way to store and manage critical information. It ensures data integrity and facilitates relational operations so you can perform complex queries, generate reports, and derive meaningful insights. Relational databases, such as Azure SQL Database, provide robust and scalable solutions for storing and processing structured data in a structured query language.

> **NEED MORE REVIEW?** **STRUCTURED DATA**
>
> You can learn more about structured data at *learn.microsoft.com/en-us/training/modules/explore-core-data-concepts/2-data-formats.*

Describe features of semi-structured data

Semi-structured data represents information that does not adhere to a rigid, predefined schema like structured data. It offers flexibility and accommodates varying formats, making it well-suited for capturing diverse attributes and evolving data structures. Unlike structured data, semi-structured data does not require fixed columns or tables. Instead, it uses formats such as JavaScript Object Notation (JSON) or eXtensible Markup Language (XML) to organize data in a hierarchical or nested structure.

Figure 1-1 shows an example of a semi-structured data document in JSON format that represents a social media post by the user JohnDoe123. The document contains fields for the author's username, the timestamp of the post, the content of the post, and the number of likes received. Additionally, there is an array of comments, with each comment containing the author's username, timestamp, and content. The flexible structure allows for optional fields or additional metadata, depending on the specific post, which means you can capture varying data attributes without the need to alter the underlying structure.

```
{
  "author": "JohnDoe123",
  "timestamp": "2023-05-16T10:30:00Z",
  "content": "Just had the most amazing hiking adventure! The views were breathtaking! 🏔️🥾 #Nature #Adventure",
  "likes": 102,
  "comments": [
    {
      "author": "JaneSmith456",
      "timestamp": "2023-05-16T11:15:00Z",
      "content": "Wow, those pictures are stunning! I need to visit that place someday. 😊"
    },
    {
      "author": "SamJones789",
      "timestamp": "2023-05-16T11:30:00Z",
      "content": "I'm so jealous! Hiking is my favorite activity. Can you share more details about the trail?"
    }
  ]
}
```

FIGURE 1-1 JSON representing semi-structured data

> **NOTE** **EXPLORING SEMI-STRUCTURED DATA REPRESENTATION**
>
> *JSON is just one of several ways in which you can represent semi-structured data.*

Semi-structured data is commonly encountered in various domains, including social media feeds, sensor data from IoT devices, and log files. With semi-structured data, businesses can capture and store diverse data sources that may have evolving schemas or complex relations.

To effectively manage and process semi-structured data, you can use specialized databases known as NoSQL (for "not only SQL" or "no SQL") databases. These databases, such as Azure Cosmos DB, provide scalable solutions for storing and querying semi-structured data. They offer flexibility and adaptability, making them suitable for handling diverse data formats and evolving schemas.

NEED MORE REVIEW?   **SEMI-STRUCTURED DATA**

You can learn more about semi-structured data at *learn.microsoft.com/en-us/training/ modules/explore-core-data-concepts/2-data-formats*.

Describe features of unstructured data

Unstructured data represents a vast and diverse category of information that lacks a pre-defined structure or format. It includes data in its rawest form, such as text documents, images, audio files, videos, and more. Unlike structured or semi-structured data, unstructured data does not fit neatly into tables or schemas, making it challenging to organize and analyze using traditional methods.

Data can encompass textual documents such as emails, news articles, or social media posts. It can also include images, such as photographs or scanned documents, audio recordings, and videos. Unstructured data may not have a consistent layout or specific attributes, making it difficult to extract insights using conventional data processing techniques.

In the example shown in Figure 1-2, each post represents an unstructured piece of data. The content varies from user to user, and there is no predefined structure or format governing the posts. Users can freely express their thoughts and emotions and use hashtags, mentions, or other forms of expression.

Effectively managing and deriving value from unstructured data requires specialized tools and techniques. Technologies such as natural language processing (NLP), image recognition, and audio transcription play a significant role in analyzing and extracting meaningful information from unstructured data sources.

In today's digital landscape, unstructured data is prevalent due to the exponential growth of internet, social media, and multimedia content. You can leverage unstructured data for sentiment analysis, customer feedback analysis, image recognition applications, and more. However, its sheer volume and lack of predefined structure pose significant challenges in terms of storage, processing, and analysis.

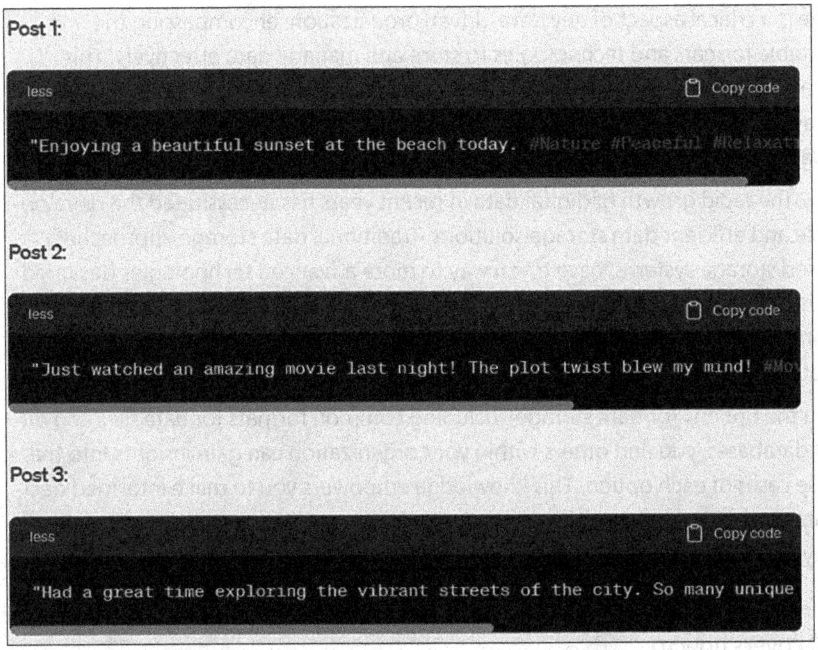

Post 1:

```less
                                                              📋 Copy code
  "Enjoying a beautiful sunset at the beach today. #Nature #Peaceful #Relaxat
```

Post 2:

```less
                                                              📋 Copy code
  "Just watched an amazing movie last night! The plot twist blew my mind! #Mo
```

Post 3:

```less
                                                              📋 Copy code
  "Had a great time exploring the vibrant streets of the city. So many unique
```

FIGURE 1-2 Unstructured data representation

To tackle these challenges, cloud-based storage solutions such as Azure Blob Storage provide scalable and cost-effective repositories for unstructured data. Advanced analytics platforms, such as Azure Cognitive Services, leverage machine learning algorithms to derive insights from unstructured data sources.

> **NEED MORE REVIEW?**   **UNSTRUCTURED DATA**
>
> You can learn more about unstructured data at *learn.microsoft.com/en-us/training/modules/explore-core-data-concepts/2-data-formats*.

Skill 1.2: Identify options for data storage

In the modern era of data-driven decision-making, you face a multitude of choices when it comes to storing your valuable data. This skill dives into the realm of data storage options, providing you insights into the various formats and technologies available. By understanding the different options for data storage, you can make informed decisions that align with your organization's specific needs, ensuring efficient data management, scalability, and reliability. Let's embark on a journey to explore the landscape of data storage, where choices abound and the right storage solution can pave the way for you to unlock the true potential of your data assets.

Data storage is a critical aspect of any data-driven organization, encompassing the selection of suitable formats and technologies to store and manage data effectively. This section delves into data storage options, providing you with a comprehensive understanding of the choices available. From traditional file formats to modern database systems, the landscape of data storage is diverse and evolving.

Contextually, the rapid growth of digital data in recent years has necessitated the development of scalable and efficient data storage solutions. Traditional data storage approaches, such as file-based storage systems, have given way to more advanced technologies designed to handle the ever-increasing volume, velocity, and variety of data. You need to consider factors such as data access speed, scalability, security, and cost-effectiveness when selecting the appropriate data storage solution.

By exploring the options for data storage, including common formats for data files and different types of databases, you and others within your organization can gain insights into the benefits and use cases of each option. This knowledge empowers you to make informed decisions about data storage that align with your organization's specific requirements, ensuring data availability, reliability, and accessibility in a rapidly evolving data landscape.

> **This skill covers how to:**
> - Describe common formats for data files
> - Describe types of databases

Describe common formats for data files

In this vast world of data storage, selecting the appropriate file format is essential for efficient data management and interoperability. Exploring the common formats of data files sheds light on their characteristics and use cases. By understanding these formats, you can make informed decisions about storing and exchanging your data to ensure seamless integration and accessibility across different systems and platforms.

Delimited file format

Delimited file formats are widely used for storing and exchanging tabular data, where fields are separated by specific delimiter characters. These formats offer you simplicity, versatility, and compatibility with various system and applications. In a delimited file, each record is represented as a line, and individual fields within the record are separated by a delimiter character, such as a comma, tab, or pipe. Let's explore the characteristics and benefits of delimited file formats.

Figure 1-3 shows an example of the comma-separated values (CSV) file format, where each line represents an employee record. The fields of each record, such as name, age, job title, and location, are separated by commas. Each comma (or delimiter) acts as a marker to distinguish one field from the other.

```
John Doe, 35 ,Software Engineer,New York
Jane Smith, 28 ,Data Analyst,San Francisco
Mark Johnson, 42 ,Project Manager,Chicago
```

FIGURE 1-3 CSV file format

The first line of a CSV file typically serves as a header, specifying the name of the fields. Subsequent lines contain the actual data, with each field representing a specific attribute of the field. With delimited files, you can easily import/export the data into various software applications and seamlessly exchange data between different systems.

Delimited file formats offer you several advantages. They are human-readable and widely supported, making them accessible across different platforms and programming languages. Because of the simplicity of the format, users can easily process and manipulate data using various tools. Delimited files are also lightweight and space-efficient, as they do not require complex data structures or encoding schemas.

These formats are commonly used for data interchange, data migration, and integration between different systems. They provide a standardized and straightforward approach to represent tabular data. While CSV is the most prevalent delimited format, other variations such as tab-separated values (TSV) and pipe-separated values (PSV) offer alternative delimiters for specific use cases.

> **NEED MORE REVIEW?   DELIMITED TEXT FILES**
>
> You can learn more about delimited text files at *learn.microsoft.com/en-us/training/modules/explore-core-data-concepts/3-file-storage*.

JavaScript Object Notation file format

JSON is a widely used file format for representing and exchanging structured data. It provides a lightweight, human-readable, and platform-independent format that is easy to parse and generate. JSON files use a hierarchical structure with key-value pairs to represent complex data structures. Let's explore the characteristics and benefits of the JSON file format.

Figure 1-4 shows a JSON file that stores information about employees in a company. The file consists of key-value pairs, with each pair representing a specific attribute of an employee. The structure allows for nesting and therefore can represent complex data relationships. An employee's record might include attributes such as name, position, department, salary, and more. Nested objects could contain additional information such as address or skills.

```
{
"_comment": "Employee 1",
"employees": [
{
"id": 1,
"name": "John Doe",
"position": "Software Engineer",
"department": "Engineering",
"salary": 75000,
"join_date": "2022-01-15"
},
{
"_comment": "Employee 2",
"id": 2,
"name": "Jane Smith",
"position": "Marketing Manager",
"department": "Marketing",
"salary": 85000,
"join_date": "2021-06-10"
},
{
    "_comment": "Employee 3",
"id": 3,
"name": "Michael Johnson",
"position": "Sales Representative",
"department": "Sales",
"salary": 60000,
"join_date": "2022-03-01"
}
]
}
```

FIGURE 1-4 JSON file format representation

NOTE **UNLOCKING THE POWER OF JSON**

JSON files offer several advantages. They are easily readable by both humans and machines, facilitating data understanding and manipulation. The format is supported by a wide range of programming language and frameworks, making it highly interoperable. JSON's hierarchical structure can represent complex data structures, making it suitable for a variety of use cases.

JSON files are commonly used for data interchange between web-based systems and APIs. They are the preferred format for transmitting structured data over HTTP requests and responses. Additionally, JSON is frequently used for configuration files, log files, and data storage in NoSQL databases because of its flexibility and ease of use.

NEED MORE REVIEW? **JAVASCRIPT OBJECT NOTATION**

You can learn more about the JSON file format at *learn.microsoft.com/en-us/training/ modules/explore-core-data-concepts/3-file-storage*.

XML data format

XML is a versatile file format used for storing and exchanging structured data. It provides a hierarchical structure using tags to define elements and using attributes to describe element properties. XML files are human-readable, platform-independent, and widely supported, making them suitable for a variety of applications.

Take, for instance, an XML file that stores information about books in a library, as shown in Figure 1-5. Each book is represented as an XML element, with nested elements representing different attributes such as title, author, genre, and more. XML allows for flexible nesting and customization and therefore can represent complex data structures and relationships.

```xml
<library>
  <book>
    <title>The Great Gatsby</title>
    <author>F. Scott Fitzgerald</author>
    <genre>Classic</genre>
    <publication_year>1925</publication_year>
    <isbn>9780743273565</isbn>
  </book>
  <book>
    <title>To Kill a Mockingbird</title>
    <author>Harper Lee</author>
    <genre>Classic</genre>
    <publication_year>1960</publication_year>
    <isbn>9780060935467</isbn>
  </book>
  <book>
    <title>The Catcher in the Rye</title>
    <author>J.D. Salinger</author>
    <genre>Coming-of-age</genre>
    <publication_year>1951</publication_year>
    <isbn>9780316769488</isbn>
  </book>
</library>
```

FIGURE 1-5 The XML file format

XML files offer several advantages. They are easily readable and understandable by both humans and machines. The hierarchical structure of XML facilitates the representation of structured and semi-structured data, making it suitable for diverse use cases. XML files are also self-descriptive, as the tags and attributes provide meaningful metadata about the data they represent.

XML is widely supported by programming languages, databases, and web technologies, making it highly interoperable. It is commonly used for exchanging data, writing configuration files, and processing complex data structures in various domains such as web services, content management systems, and scientific research.

Parquet file format

Parquet is a columnar storage file format designed for efficient data processing and analytics in big data environments. It provides a highly optimized and compressed representation of structured data, making it well-suited for handling large datasets. Parquet files organize data by columns rather than rows and therefore support advanced column pruning and predicate push-down optimizations.

Figure 1-6 shows a Parquet file that stores sales data for an e-commerce business. Instead of storing all the attributes of a sale in row-based format, Parquet stores each column of data separately. This columnar organization allows for efficient compression and encoding techniques specific to each column, reducing storage requirements and improving query performance. The example shown contains these columns: OrderID, CustomerID, ProductID, Quantity, Price, and Timestamp.

```
File: transactions.parquet

Schema:
- OrderID: Integer
- CustomerID: Integer
- ProductID: Integer
- Quantity: Integer
- Price: Double
- Timestamp: Timestamp

Data:
[
    {"OrderID": 1, "CustomerID": 101, "ProductID": 5001, "Quantity": 2, "Price": 49.99, "Timestamp": "2023-05-15T10:30:00"},
    {"OrderID": 2, "CustomerID": 102, "ProductID": 5002, "Quantity": 1, "Price": 149.99, "Timestamp": "2023-05-15T11:45:00"},
    {"OrderID": 3, "CustomerID": 103, "ProductID": 5003, "Quantity": 4, "Price": 9.99, "Timestamp": "2023-05-16T09:15:00"}
]
```

FIGURE 1-6 The Parquet file format

Parquet files offer several advantages. The columnar storage format reduces disk I/O and improves query performance, especially when queries involve only a subset of columns. Parquet leverages advanced compression techniques, such as run-length encoding (RLE) and dictionary encoding, to further reduce the storage footprint while maintaining data integrity. The format also supports nested and complex data types and therefore can represent hierarchical structures.

Parquet is widely adopted in big data processing frameworks such as Apache Hadoop and Apache Spark, as it accelerates analytics workloads by efficiently reading and processing only the required columns. Its compatibility with various data processing tools makes it a preferred choice for high-performance data analytics and data warehousing scenarios.

Avro file format

When it comes to storing and exchanging structured data efficiently, the Avro file format stands out as a compact and dynamic solution. Embracing a binary encoding approach, Avro files offer high-performance data processing and storage capabilities. What sets Avro apart is its ability to provide a self-describing schema alongside the data, facilitating schema evolution and dynamic typing.

Figure 1-7 shows an example of the Avro schema defining the structure of the user profile data. The type field specifies that it is a record, the name is User Profile, and the fields are defined in the fields array. In this case, the fields include the user's name (string), age (int), location (string), and interests (an array of strings).

```
{
    "type": "record",
    "name": "UserProfile",
    "fields": [
        {"name": "name", "type": "string"},
        {"name": "age", "type": "int"},
        {"name": "location", "type": "string"},
        {"name": "interests", "type": {"type": "array", "items": "string"}}
    ]
}
```

FIGURE 1-7 The Avro file format

Within this file, both the data and its accompanying schema are encapsulated. This inclusion empowers flexibility, allowing the schema to evolve over time without compromising compatibility with existing data. The schema is a rich and diverse representation of structured information.

Avro files offer remarkable advantages. Through their binary encoding, these files achieve exceptional compactness and efficiency, making them ideal for managing and transmitting large volumes of data. The self-describing nature of Avro allows seamless schema evolution, facilitating the adaptation to changing data requirements. Additionally, Avro supports complex data structures, including nested and hierarchical relationships, and therefore can represent intricate information models.

With its outstanding performance, flexibility, and schema evolution capabilities, the Avro file format has garnered widespread adoption within big data processing frameworks such as Apache Hadoop and Apache Spark. Its ability to efficiently handle high-volume data processing, analytics, and seamless interoperability between systems positions Avro as a powerful and dynamic choice.

> **NOTE** **EMPOWERING DATA STORAGE**
>
> When exploring the features of the Avro file format, it's important to note the following:
>
> - Avro supports popular compression codecs such as Snappy, Deflate, and Bzip2.
>
> - You can define an Avro schema using JSON.

> **NEED MORE REVIEW?** **AVRO FILE FORMAT**
>
> You can learn more about the Avro file format at *learn.microsoft.com/en-us/training/modules/ explore-core-data-concepts/3-file-storage*.

ORC file format

The optimized row columnar (ORC) file format is designed to optimize performance and storage efficiency for big analytics. It leverages columnar storage and advance compression techniques to deliver high-speed data processing and a reduced storage footprint.

Let's say you have an ORC file that stores sales data for an e-commerce company. Instead of storing data in a row-by-row format, ORC organizes the data into columns, as shown in Figure 1-8.

- Each column contains data of a specific type (e.g., integers, strings, dates).
- Data within each column is stored together, which allows for efficient compression and encoding.
- Rows are typically stored in *stripes* for further compression and optimization.

ORC files offer several advantages. The columnar storage approach reduces disk I/O by reading only the necessary columns during data processing, resulting in faster query performance. Additionally, ORC utilizes advanced compression techniques, such as RLE, dictionary encoding, and bloom filters, to minimize storage requirements while maintaining data integrity. These optimizations make ORC a highly efficient format for big data analytics and data warehousing.

The OCR file format is widely adopted in big data ecosystems, including Apache Hadoop and Apache Hive. Its compatibility with various data processing tools and frameworks makes it a popular choice for optimizing data processing pipelines. By leveraging the benefits of ORC, you can achieve significant performance gains and storage savings when dealing with large-scale data analytics.

```
+------------------------------------+
| Column1 (e.g., CustomerID)         |
|------------------------------------|
| 12345                              |
| 56789                              |
| 10111                              |
| ...                                |
+------------------------------------+


+------------------------------------+
| Column2 (e.g., ProductID)          |
|------------------------------------|
| 789                                |
| 456                                |
| 123                                |
| ...                                |
+------------------------------------+


+------------------------------------+
| Column3 (e.g., Quantity)           |
|------------------------------------|
| 5                                  |
| 2                                  |
| 10                                 |
| ...                                |
+------------------------------------+


+------------------------------------+
| Column4 (e.g., OrderDate)          |
|------------------------------------|
| 2023-01-15                         |
| 2023-02-10                         |
| 2023-03-05                         |
| ...                                |
+------------------------------------+
```

FIGURE 1-8 The ORC file format

> **NEED MORE REVIEW?** **OPTIMIZED ROW COLUMNAR FORMAT**
>
> You can learn more about the ORC format at *learn.microsoft.com/en-us/training/modules/explore-core-data-concepts/3-file-storage*.

Describe types of databases

Effective data management is essential in today's world, where information fuels innovation and drives business success. Choosing the right database type plays a pivotal role in storing, retrieving, and analyzing data with efficiency and precision. Let's journey through the realm of database types, where you will explore the diverse options available and their specific use cases. By gaining a deep understanding of these database types, you can make informed decisions that align with your unique data requirements and unlock the true potential of your data assets. Get ready to embark on an exploration of the vast landscape of databases, where choices abound and where the right selection can pave the way for streamlined data management and impactful analytics.

The rapid growth of digital data in recent years has led to the development of various database types, each tailored to address specific needs and data characteristics. In the context of the DP-900 exam, it is essential to have a comprehensive understanding of the characteristics, strengths, and use cases of different database types. Whether it's the structured precision of relational databases, the flexibility of NoSQL databases, or the cloud-native capabilities of Azure databases, the right database choice sets the foundation for successful data management and empowers organizations to harness the full potential of their data assets.

Relational database

Relational databases are a cornerstone of modern business data management, providing a structured and efficient approach to organizing and manipulating data. From customer information to financial transactions, relational databases offer a robust foundation for businesses to store, retrieve, and analyze their critical data.

Relational databases organize data into tables, where each table consists of rows and columns. This tabular structure allows businesses to represent entities and their relationships in a clear and organized manner. For example, consider a customer database table with columns such as Customer ID, Name, Email, and Phone Number. Each row represents a specific customer, and the columns store their corresponding attributes. With this structured representation, users can retrieve data efficiently and write complex queries using SQL.

Relational databases offer several advantages for businesses. First, they ensure data consistency and integrity by enforcing relationships between tables through keys and constraints. This reliability means users get accurate reporting, regulatory compliance, and trustworthy decision-making. Second, relational databases support transactional processing, allowing businesses to perform reliable and secure operations on their data, such as creating, updating, and deleting records. This is crucial for maintaining data accuracy and auditability.

Furthermore, relational databases provide powerful query capabilities so that businesses can extract valuable insights from their data. SQL queries can be crafted to join multiple tables, filter databases on specific criteria, aggregate information, and perform complex calculations. This ability to efficiently retrieve and analyze data empowers businesses to make data-driven decisions and gain a competitive edge.

Relational databases have been widely adopted across industries and are supported by a variety of database management systems (DBMSs) such as Microsoft SQL Server, Oracle Database, and MySQL. These systems provide robust features for data storage, indexing performance optimization, and security.

> **NEED MORE REVIEW? RELATIONAL DATABASES**
>
> You can learn more about relational databases at *learn.microsoft.com/en-us/training/ modules/explore-core-data-concepts/4-databases.*

Non-relational databases

Non-relational databases, also known as NoSQL databases, have emerged as powerful alternatives to traditional relationship databases for businesses. These databases provide a flexible and scalable approach to storing and managing a vast amount of unstructured and semi-structured data. Let's explore the key aspects and benefits of non-relational databases from a business perspective.

Non-relational databases offer a variety of data models, including document databases, key-value stores, columnar databases, and graph databases. Each data model is designed to address specific data needs and use cases, providing businesses with the flexibility to adapt to diverse data structures.

Consider a business that operates an e-commerce platform. A document database could be used to store customer profiles, where each customer's data is represented as a document containing attributes such as Name, Email, Address, and Purchase History. This flexibility document structure allows for easily storing and retrieving customer information even while accommodating variations in data formats.

Non-relational databases provide several advantages for businesses. First, they offer horizontal scalability, allowing businesses to handle massive data volumes and high-velocity data streams. These databases are built to distribute data across multiple servers and therefore offer seamless scalability as data requirements grow. This scalability supports businesses in handling dynamic workloads and accommodating evolving data demands.

Second, non-relational databases excel in handling unstructured and semi-structured data. They offer schema-less designs, allowing for flexibility in data modeling and accommodating changing data structures over time. This flexibility is crucial in scenarios where data structures are not predefined or where data formats vary greatly.

Furthermore, non-relational databases are highly performant, which results in fast data retrieval and processing. They often employ distributed computing techniques and optimized data storage mechanisms to deliver real-time data access and analytics capabilities. This performance advantage contributes to efficient decision-making and empowers businesses to derive meaningful insight from their data.

Non-relational databases have gained significant traction in modern business environments and are supported by popular systems such as Azure Cosmo DB, MongoDB, and Cassandra, just to name a few. These systems provide robust features for data storage, scalability, and distributed computing.

In a nutshell, non-relational databases offer businesses the flexibility, scalability, and performance required to handle diverse and rapidly growing data. With their ability to handle unstructured data and adapt to changing requirements, non-relational databases empower businesses to unlock the full potential of their data assets.

NEED MORE REVIEW? **NON-RELATIONAL DATABASES**

You can learn more about non-relational databases at *learn.microsoft.com/en-us/training/ modules/explore-core-data-concepts/4-databases.*

Cloud databases

Cloud databases have revolutionized the way businesses store, manage, and analyze their data. These databases leverage the power of cloud computing, offering scalability, flexibility, and ease of management.

With cloud databases, businesses can store and access their data in the cloud, eliminating the need for on-premises infrastructure and maintenance. By leveraging cloud services, businesses can focus on their core competencies while benefiting from the scalability and agility provided by cloud databases.

An example of a cloud database service is Microsoft Azure SQL Database. It offers a fully managed, scalable, and secure database platform so that businesses can rapidly provision and scale their databases based on demand. With Azure SQL Database, businesses can focus on their applications and data, leaving the infrastructure management to the cloud provider.

Cloud databases provide several advantages for businesses. First, they offer scalability, allowing businesses to scale their databases up or down based on workload demands. This flexibility ensures optimal performance and cost efficiency, as resources can be allocated as needed. Businesses can easily handle spikes in user activity or accommodate data growth without significant infrastructure investments.

Second, cloud databases enhance agility and collaboration. They provide seamless access to data from anywhere, which means geographically distributed teams can work together effectively. Cloud-based collaboration and integration tools further streamline workflows and facilitate real-time decision-making, boosting business productivity and efficiency.

Cloud databases also have robust security measures and compliance capabilities. Cloud providers invest heavily in security infrastructure, implementing stringent access controls, encryption, and continuous monitoring to protect business data. Compliance certifications such as International Organization for Standardization (ISO) 2700, the Health Insurance Portability and Accountability Act (HIPAA), and General Data Protection Regulation (GDPR) demonstrate adherence to industry standards and regulatory requirements, providing peace of mind for businesses.

Furthermore, with cloud databases, businesses can leverage advanced analytics and machine learning capabilities. Cloud providers offer integrated analytics services, such as Azure Synapse Analytics, so businesses can derive actionable insights from their data. These services provide powerful tools for data exploration, visualization, and predictive analytics, driving data-driven decision-making and enhancing business competitiveness.

Cloud databases are supported by leading cloud providers, including Microsoft Azure, Amazon Web Services (AWS), and Google Cloud Platform (GCP). These providers offer a wide range of database options, including relational, NoSQL, and specialized databases, tailored to meet diverse business needs. These cloud databases empower businesses by providing scalable, agile, and secure data management solutions. With their ability to scale on demand, foster collaboration, ensure data security, and provide advanced analytics, cloud databases are integral to driving business growth and innovation in the digital era.

Skill 1.3: Describe common data workloads

In the dynamic world of data management, understanding common data workloads is essential for data professionals seeking to harness the transformative potential of data. This skill explores the realm of common data workloads, providing insights into different types of data processing scenarios and their specific requirements. By gaining a deep understanding of these workloads, individuals can effectively design and implement data solutions that align with business needs and drive meaningful insights. Let's take a look at some common data workloads and unlock the work power of data.

In today's data-driven landscape, organizations encounter two primary types of data workloads: transactional workloads and analytical workloads. Transactional workloads focus on the efficient and reliable processing of business transactions, such as capturing customer orders, processing financial transactions, or updating inventory levels. These workloads require strong data consistency, durability, and atomicity/consistency/isolation/durability (ACID) properties to ensure data integrity and reliability.

On the other hand, analytical workloads revolve around deriving insights and knowledge from data support decision-making and strategic planning. Analytical workloads involve complex queries, aggregations, data transformations, and statistical analysis to uncover patterns, trends, and correlations within the data. These workloads typically require scalable processing power, efficient data retrieval, and advanced analytics capabilities to unlock valuable insights and drive informed decisions.

As data volumes continue to grow exponentially and organizations increasingly rely on data-driven insights, understanding and effectively managing these common data workloads become paramount. By comprehending the distinct requirements and characteristics of transactional and analytical workloads, individuals can design appropriate data architectures, select suitable database systems, and implement robust data processing solutions to meet business objectives.

This book delves into the intricacies of these common data workloads, ensuring that data professionals process the knowledge and skills necessary to navigate the dynamic world of data management. By grasping the nuances of transactional and analytical workloads, individuals can contribute to the design and implementation of efficient data solutions, paving the way for business success in an increasingly data-centric era.

This skill covers how to:
- Describe features of transactional workloads
- Describe features of analytical workloads

Describe features of transactional workloads

Transactional workloads play a critical role in ensuring the smooth operation of businesses and maintaining data integrity. These workloads encompass activities such as capturing customer orders, processing financial transactions, and updating inventory levels.

Transactional workloads are designed to handle business operations that involve data modifications, ensuring the accuracy, consistency, and reliability of data. Let's consider an e-commerce platform that processes customer orders. Each customer order represents a transaction that requires capturing the order details, updating inventory levels, and recording the financial transaction. These transactions must be executed reliably and in an atomic manner, meaning they should either complete successfully or be rolled back entirely if an error occurs.

Transactional workloads offer several advantages for business. First, they ensure data consistency and integrity. The ACID properties guide transactional processing, ensuring that data remains in a consistent state even in the event of failure or concurrent access. This integrity is crucial for financial systems, inventory management, and other critical business functions.

Second, transactional workloads support concurrency control and isolation in a multiuser environment, where multiple transactions can occur simultaneously. Transactional processing mechanisms ensure that transactions are executed independently and do not interfere with each other, maintaining data integrity and preventing conflicts.

Furthermore, transactional workloads facilitate data durability and reliability. Transactional systems employ techniques such as write-ahead logging and database recovery mechanisms to ensure that committed transactions persist even in the face of system failures. This durability ensures that critical business operations can be restored and recovered without data loss.

Transactional workloads are supported by various database systems such as relational databases, where ACID properties are typically enforced. These systems provide transaction management features that guarantee data consistency, durability, and isolation. We can say transactional workloads are essential for maintaining accurate data, supporting reliable business operations, and ensuring data integrity. By executing operations in an atomic and consistent manner, businesses can confidently process customer orders, handle financial transactions, and manage inventory levels, fostering trust and reliability in their operations.

> **NEED MORE REVIEW?** **TRANSACTIONAL WORKLOADS**
>
> You can learn more about transactional workloads at *learn.microsoft.com/en-us/training/ modules/explore-core-data-concepts/5-transactional-data-processing*.

Describe features of analytical workloads

Analytical workloads play a pivotal role in extracting valuable insights and patterns from data to support informed decision-making and strategic planning within businesses. These workloads involve complex data analysis, aggregations, and transformations to uncover meaningful information.

Analytical workloads encompass a range of activities, such as data exploration, statistical analysis, data mining, and predictive modeling. The process begins by identifying relevant data sources and extracting the required data. The advanced analytics techniques, such as data visualization, machine learning, and statistical algorithms, are applied to gain insights and patterns from the data. The results are interpreted and translated into actionable business intelligence, which results in data-driven decision-making.

Analytical workloads serve different data personas within organizations.

- **Data analysts:** Data analysts leverage analytical workloads to explore and analyze data, uncovering trends, correlations, and patterns that provide valuable insights. They use statistical techniques and data visualization tools to communicate their findings effectively to stakeholders, resulting in evidence-based decision-making.

- **Data scientists:** Data scientists go beyond analyzing data and utilize advanced analytical methods to develop predictive models, machine learning algorithms, and data-driven solutions. They leverage analytical workloads to build models that forecast future trends, identify opportunities, and optimize business processes.

- **Business executives:** Business executives rely on analytical workloads to gain high-level insight and make strategic decisions. They rely on reports, dashboards, and visualizations generated by analytical workloads to monitor key performance indicators, track business metrics, and assess the effectiveness of strategies.

- **Data engineers:** Data engineers support analytical workloads by designing and implementing the data infrastructure necessary for data analysis. They ensure that data is ingested, processed, and made available in a format that facilitates efficient analysis. They collaborate with data analysts and scientists to ensure data quality and reliability.

Analytical workloads are supported by various technologies and tools, including data platforms, machine learning frameworks, and business intelligence tools. These solutions provide capabilities for data exploration, modeling, visualization, and advanced analytics.

> **NEED MORE REVIEW?** **ANALYTICAL WORKLOAD**
>
> You can learn more about analytical workloads at *learn.microsoft.com/en-us/training/ modules/explore-core-data-concepts/6-analytical-processing*.

Skill 1.4: Identify roles and responsibilities for data workloads

This section focuses on the critical aspect of identifying roles and responsibilities for data workloads. In the world of data management, different professionals contribute their expertise to ensure the efficient handling, processing, and utilization of data. Understanding these roles and responsibilities is vital for organizations to effectively manage and leverage their data assets.

In today's data-driven landscape, organizations rely on dedicated professionals to fulfill specific roles related to data management. This skill highlights the significance of recognizing and assigning the appropriate roles within data workloads. By identifying the individuals responsible for specific tasks, organizations can streamline their data operations, promote collaboration, and optimize the overall data management process.

Assigning roles and responsibilities for data workloads ensures that the right expertise is applied to each aspect of data management. Database and administrators, data engineers, and data analysts play pivotal roles in supporting data workloads, each with their unique skill sets and responsibilities.

Identifying these roles helps establish clear line of responsibility and accountability. By understanding and assigning these roles, organizations can foster collaboration and coordination among professionals involved in data workloads. This alignment promotes effective data management, offers smooth data workflows, and maximizes the value derived from data assets.

This exam skill emphasizes the importance of recognizing these roles and responsibilities in the broader context of data workloads. By understanding the significance of each role and its contribution to successful data management, individuals can grasp the collaborative efforts required to leverage data effectively. Let's take a closer look at each of these data roles and their responsibilities.

This skill covers how to:

- Describe responsibilities for database administrators
- Describe responsibilities for data engineers
- Describe responsibilities for data analysts

Describe responsibilities for database administrators

As a database administrator (DBA), your role is crucial in the management and maintenance of databases, ensuring their smooth operation, integrity, and performance. You are the guardian of data within your organization, responsible for various tasks that contribute to efficiently storing, retrieving, and securing data.

You are involved in the entire life cycle of databases, starting from the initial design and creation to ongoing maintenance and optimization. You work closely with stakeholders to understand data requirements and design database structures that optimize performance and scalability. You determine data models, create database schemas, and define relationships between tables.

Ensuring data security is a critical aspect of your role. You implement access controls, user authentication, and encryption mechanisms to protect sensitive data from unauthorized access or malicious activities. You establish backup and recovery procedures to safeguard against data loss, ensuring the continuity of business operations.

Monitoring databases and optimizing performance are essential responsibilities. You constantly monitor database performance, identifying and resolving bottlenecks to enhance system efficiency. You analyze query performance, tune database configurations, and optimize indexing strategies to improve overall performance and ensure timely data retrieval.

Your expertise also extends to backup and recovery. You design and implement robust backup and recovery strategies to protect data from system failure, human errors, or disasters. You schedule regular backups, perform restoration tests, and maintain disaster recovery plans to ensure data availability and minimize downtime.

Keeping databases up to date is another aspect of your role. You oversee database upgrades and apply patches, ensuring that the database systems are equipped with the latest features, bug fixes, and security updates. You perform compatibility tests and ensure seamless transitions to new versions or releases.

Your role as a DBA is instrumental in maintaining data integrity, ensuring system availability, and supporting business continuity. Your expertise ensures that databases operate efficiently, adhere to industry standards, and meet regulatory requirements. With your skills and knowledge, you contribute to the data-driven systems within your organization functioning smoothly.

> **NEED MORE REVIEW?** **DATABASE ADMINISTRATORS**
>
> You can learn more about data administrators at *learn.microsoft.com/en-us/training/modules/explore-roles-responsibilities-world-of-data/2-explore-job-roles*.

Describe responsibilities for data engineers

As a data engineer, your role is vital in designing, constructing, and maintaining the data infrastructure and pipeline to promote efficient data processing and analysis. You play a crucial part in the data management process, ensuring that data flows seamlessly across systems and remains accessible for analysis.

Your primary responsibility is to design and construct the data infrastructure necessary for effective data management. You collaborate with stakeholders to understand their data requirements, identify relevant data sources, and determine the best approach to data integration. You develop data pipelines, ensuring the smooth and reliable flow of data from the source systems to the target destinations.

You are involved in data ingestion, where you extract data from various sources such as databases, files, or APIs. You transform and cleanse the data to ensure its quality and consistency, making it suitable for downstream analysis. This may involve tasks such as data extraction, data validation, data cleansing, and data enrichment.

In addition to data ingestion, you are responsible for data transformation and integration. You apply data processing techniques to convert raw data into a usable format, ensuring it aligns with the required data model's schema. This may involve tasks such as data aggregations, data filtering, data normalization, and data enrichment.

Data engineering also involves developing data processing workflows. You design and implement efficient workflows that orchestrate the movement and transformation of data, ensuring optimal performance and reliability. This may include using workflow management tools or frameworks to schedule and monitor data processing tasks.

An example of your role as a data engineer could be working on a project to develop a real-time analytics platform for a financial institution. You would be responsible for designing and implementing the data infrastructure, ingesting real-time transaction data from multiple sources, transforming and aggregating the data, and making it available for real-time analysis and reporting.

Your expertise in data engineering contributes to the overall success of data-driven initiatives within your organization. By building robust data pipelines, ensuring data quality and reliability, and implementing efficient data processing, you facilitate effective data analysis and drive actionable insights.

> **NEED MORE REVIEW?** **DATA ENGINEER**
>
> You can learn more about data engineers at *learn.microsoft.com/en-us/training/modules/ explore-roles-responsibilities-world-of-data/2-explore-job-roles.*

Describe responsibilities for data analysts

As a data analyst, your role is crucial in uncovering valuable insight and patterns within data to support informed decision-making within your organization. You play a pivotal role in analyzing, interpreting, and visualizing the data to derive meaningful information that drives business strategies. Let's explore your comprehensive role as a data analyst from a business perspective.

Your primary responsibility is to explore and analyze data to uncover trends, correlations, and patterns that provide valuable insights. You work with various data sources, ranging from structured databases to unstructured text files, and use statistical techniques and analytical tools to extract meaningful information.

Data exploration is an essential part of your role. You dive deep into the data, examining its structure, quality, and relationships. You identify relevant variable and metrics to analyze, ensuring that the data is appropriate for the questions or problems at hand.

Once you have gathered and cleaned the data, you apply statistical analysis techniques to identify patterns and relationships. You may perform tasks such as descriptive statistics, hypothesis testing, regression analysis, or clustering to extract insights from the data. These analyses help you uncover trends, anomalies, and relationships that can guide decision-making.

Data visualization is another crucial aspect of your role. You use visual tools and techniques to present data in a clear and concise manner. By creating charts, graphs, and dashboards, you transform complex datasets into easily understandable visual representations. These visualizations help stakeholders to grasp insights quickly and make informed decisions.

An example of your role as a data analyst is analyzing customer behavior data for an e-commerce company. You would examine the data to understand customer preferences, identify purchasing patterns, and segment customers based on their buying behaviors. These insights would then inform marketing strategies, product recommendations, and customer retention efforts.

Your expertise as a data analyst contributes to evidence-based decision-making within your organization. By analyzing and interpreting data, you provide insights that support strategic planning, optimize operations, and drive business growth.

> **NEED MORE REVIEW?** **DATA ANALYSTS**
>
> You can learn more about data analysts at *learn.microsoft.com/en-us/training/modules/explore-roles-responsibilities-world-of-data/2-explore-job-roles*.

EXAM TIP

When preparing for the exam, you should focus on understanding the core data concepts and their practical application. Familiarize yourself with different data representation formats, storage options, and common data workloads. Pay attention to the roles and responsibilities of database administrators, data engineers, and data analysts. Additionally, practice relating these concepts to real-world scenarios to reinforce your understanding. Being able to apply your knowledge to practical situations will help you excel on the exam and in real-world data management scenarios.

Chapter summary

- Data concepts
  - Data can be represented as structured, semi-structured, or unstructured.
  - There are various ways to store data, which include common file formats and different types of databases.
  - It's essential to understand the difference between transactional and analytical data workloads.
- Roles and responsibilities
  - Database administrators are responsible for managing and maintaining databases.
  - Data engineers play a pivotal role in building and maintaining the data infrastructure.
  - Data analysts primarily focus on extracting valuable insights and analyzing data to inform decisions.

- Key takeaways
  - The representation of data can vary widely depending on its structure and format.
  - Options for data storage range from various file formats to databases.
  - Transactional analytical workloads process unique and distinct characteristics.
  - Several roles work in tandem to ensure the effective management and utilization of data.

Thought experiment

In this thought experiment, demonstrate your skills and knowledge of the topics covered in this chapter. You can find answers to this thought experiment in the next section.

1. Your company is planning to implement a new database system to handle its growing customer data. Who among the following roles is primarily responsible for ensuring data security, backup, and system performance?

   A. Data engineer

   B. Database administrator

   C. Data analyst

   D. None of the above

2. Your organization is dealing with a massive influx of data from various sources and needs to design efficient data pipelines. Which role is responsible for designing and building these data pipelines?

   A. Data engineer

   B. Database administrator

   C. Data analyst

   D. All of the above

3. You need to analyze customer purchase data to identify trends and create reports for your management team. Which role is best suited for this task?

   A. Data engineer

   B. Database administrator

   C. Data analyst

   D. All of the above

4. Your organization is facing performance issues with its database system, resulting in slow query execution. Which role would you consult to optimize the database performance?

   A. Data engineer

   B. Database administrator

C.   Data analyst

D.   All of the above

5.   Your company wants to implement real-time analytics to track user activities on its website. Which role would be instrumental in setting up the infrastructure for real-time data processing?

A.   Data engineer

B.   Database administrator

C.   Data analyst

D.   None of the above

6.   Your organization needs to ensure data is stored securely and can be recovered in the case of disasters. Which role is responsible for setting up data backups and recovery procedures?

A.   Data engineer

B.   Database administrator

C.   Data analyst

D.   All of the above

7.   You are tasked with designing a database schema for a new project. Which role is typically responsible for this task?

A.   Data engineer

B.   Database administrator

C.   Data analyst

D.   All of the above

8.   Your company is planning to implement a data warehouse for historical data analysis. Which role would be involved in selecting and configuring data warehousing services?

A.   Data engineer

B.   Database administrator

C.   Data analyst

D.   All of the above

9.   Your organization needs to extract insights from unstructured text data. Which role is most suitable for this task?

A.   Data engineer

B.   Database administrator

C.   Data analyst

D.   All of the above

10. Your organization is expanding its use of cloud-based data services. Which role would likely be involved in selecting and implementing these cloud services?

    A. Data engineer

    B. Database administrator

    C. Data analyst

    D. All of the above

11. Your organization needs to store large volumes of structured data efficiently. Which file format is most suitable for this requirement?

    A. JSON

    B. XML

    C. Parquet

    D. ORC

12. Your team is tasked with handling semi-structured data such as log files from various sources. Which file format is designed for storing and querying semi-structured data?

    A. JSON

    B. XML

    C. Parquet

    D. Delimited text

13. Your company deals with extensive financial data and needs to ensure data consistency and eliminate data redundancy. What type of database is best suited for this requirement?

    A. Relational database

    B. Non-relational database

    C. Graph database

    D. Columnar database

14. Your organization operates in a highly regulated industry and must maintain transactional data integrity. Which type of database is essential for ensuring atomicity, consistency, isolation, and durability (ACID)?

    A. Relational database

    B. Non-relational database

    C. Columnar database

    D. Document database

15. Your company needs to store historical data for business analytics. Which data warehousing service in Azure is suitable for this requirement?

    A. Azure SQL Database

    B. Azure Cosmos DB

C. Azure Synapse Analytics

D. Azure Data Lake Storage

Thought experiment answers

This section contains the answers for the thought experiment. Each answer explains why the answer choice is correct.

1. **B** Database administrator

   Explanation: Database administrators (DBAs) are essential for maintaining the integrity, security, and performance of the database system. They oversee access controls, implement encryption, schedule regular backups, and optimize queries to ensure the database functions reliably and efficiently.

2. **A** Data engineer

   Explanation: Data engineers play a pivotal role in constructing data pipelines that retrieve data from various sources, transform it to meet specific requirements, and load it into data storage systems. Their expertise lies in maintaining data integrity, applying data transformation logic, and streamlining the flow of data for analysis. Data engineers ensure that the data is efficiently prepared for analytical processes so that businesses can derive meaningful insights from a diverse array of data sources.

3. **C** Data analyst

   Explanation: Data analysts possess the analytical expertise to examine data, apply statistical methods, and generate reports. They can identify patterns in customer behavior, extract actionable insights, and present findings to support data-driven decision-making.

4. **B** Database administrator

   Explanation: Database administrators specialize in fine-tuning database performance. They identify and resolve bottlenecks, optimize SQL queries, configure indexing, and manage system resources to ensure responsive database operations.

5. **A** Data engineer

   Explanation: Data engineers are responsible for building the infrastructure needed for real-time data processing. They design data pipelines so users can efficiently capture, process, and analyze streaming data.

6. **B** Database administrator

   Explanation: Database administrators are the primary custodians of data security and recovery. They establish robust backup and disaster recovery plans to safeguard data integrity and availability.

7. **D** All of the above

   Explanation: Database design is often a collaborative effort involving data engineers, who design the schema structure; DBAs, who ensure it meets performance and security requirements; and data analysts, who provide input on data access needs.

8. **A** Data engineer

   Explanation: Data engineers are responsible for selecting, configuring, and maintaining data warehousing services. They ensure data is stored and structured optimally for analytical purposes.

9. **C** Data analyst

   Explanation: Data analysts are skilled in natural language processing (NLP) and text analysis. They can extract valuable insights from unstructured text data, such as customer reviews or social media comments.

10. **D** All of the above

    Explanation: Cloud adoption involves multiple roles. Data engineers choose appropriate cloud-based data storage and processing solutions. DBAs ensure database integration and security in the cloud, and data analysts use cloud tools for analysis and reporting collaboration among all roles, which is crucial for a successful transition to cloud-based data services.

11. **C** Parquet

    Explanation: Parquet is a columnar storage file format that excels at storing large volumes of structured data efficiently, making it an ideal choice for such scenarios.

12. **A** JSON

    Explanation: JavaScript Object Notation (JSON) is a flexible and widely used format for storing and querying semi-structured data, making it suitable for log files and other similar data.

13. **A** Relational database

    Explanation: Relational databases are known for their data consistency, structured schema, and ability to eliminate data redundancy, making them well-suited for financial data.

14. **A** Relational database

    Explanation: Relational databases are known for their support of ACID properties, making them critical in scenarios where transactional data integrity is paramount.

15. **C** Azure Synapse Analytics

    Explanation: Azure Synapse Analytics is a powerful data warehousing service designed for historical data storage and advanced analytics.

CHAPTER 2

Identify considerations for relational data on Azure

This chapter focuses on the crucial considerations when dealing with relational data on Azure. We will explore the Azure landscape, cover its relational database services, and build upon the foundational knowledge necessary for effective data work in the Azure environment.

We'll begin this chapter with Skill 2.1 by examining core relational concepts. To comprehend Azure's approach to handling data, it is crucial to understand what relational data is and how normalization contributes to its efficient management. Next, we delve into the Structured Query Language (SQL), the ubiquitous tool you will use to interact with these databases. We'll dissect the fundamental SQL statements that are integral to data manipulation and retrieval. To finish this section, we will explore the various data objects that will be part of your daily vernacular when dealing with Azure databases.

In Skill 2.2, we transition our focus to the relational data services offered by Azure. The expansive Azure SQL family of products, with its rich set of capabilities, will be our starting point. We'll follow this with a look at SQL Server on Azure Virtual Machines and how it integrates the familiar SQL Server environment with the scalable, high-performance, and cost-effective infrastructure provided by Azure. Lastly, we will look at Azure database services tailored to open-source database systems.

By the end of this chapter, you'll have a comprehensive understanding of Azure's relational data landscape. Not only will this strengthen your preparation for the DP-900 examination, but it will provide you with valuable insights applicable to your career as a data professional.

Skills covered in this chapter:

- Skill 2.1 Describe relational concepts
- Skill 2.2 Describe relational Azure data services

Skill 2.1: Describe relational concepts

When exploring relational concepts, you will find yourself thinking about data management within the cloud-centric world of Microsoft Azure. Data management handling is indispensable for leveraging Azure's robust data services, which require a keen understanding of relational database intricacies.

Envision organizing data in a structured manner, akin to tables with rows signifying unique records and columns delineating specific attributes. This visualization encapsulates the essence of relational data, which serves as the bedrock for building, querying, and manipulating databases in a coherent and systematic fashion. Mastery of relational data concepts is imperative, as it fosters data integrity and efficiency.

Delving deeper, you encounter normalization, a methodical strategy aimed at minimizing redundancy and fortifying data integrity. Normalization is about dissecting your data, distributing it across related tables, and ensuring each piece of information resides in its rightful place. Grasping normalization's significance is paramount, as it directly influences your database's structural optimization, enhancing maintainability and expediting query performance.

As you navigate through this data-centric realm, SQL emerges as your primary tool of communication with relational databases. Learning SQL means learning the lexicon of databases, where you can retrieve, insert, update, and delete data with precision and efficiency. A standardized language across relational databases, SQL is vital for effective data management and manipulation.

Lastly, your journey brings you to database objects—diverse elements within a database that you can create, modify, and interact with. Objects range from tables and views to indexes and stored procedures, each playing a unique and crucial role in how data is structured, stored, and accessed. Understanding these components is like solving a complex puzzle; recognizing how each piece connects allows you to forge a complete, efficient, and effective database solution.

This skill covers how to:

- Identify features of relational data
- Describe normalization and why it is used
- Identify common structured query language (SQL) statements
- Identify common database objects

Identify features of relational data

Relational data refers to the type of data that can be organized into a table structure with related values connected to each other. This table structure consists of rows and columns, where each row represents a record, and each column represents a particular type of data called a *file* or *attribute*. Here are some of the key features of relational data:

- **Tables:** In a relational database, all data is stored in a table, which is structured in rows and columns. Each column represents a type of data (an attribute), and each row represents an instance of that data (a record). For example, in a Student table, columns could be StudentID, Name, and Major, while each row would represent an individual student's data.

- **Keys:** Keys are a crucial feature of relational data. A *primary key* is a unique identifier for a row in the table. *Foreign keys* establish relationships between tables. For instance, a CourseID might be a foreign key in an Enrollments table, linking it to the Courses table.

- **Normalization:** This is the process of organizing data to minimize redundancy and avoid data anomalies, such as update errors. It involves decomposing a table into less redundant tables without losing information.

- **Relationships:** The relational model allows for relations among tables, typically through foreign keys. Relationships can be one-to-one, one-to-many, or many-to-many. For example, one student (in the Student table) can be enrolled in many courses (in the Courses table); this is a one-to-many relationship.

- **Data integrity:** Relational database enforces data integrity rules, ensuring the accuracy and consistency of data. These include entity integrity (no duplicate rows), referential integrity (consistency across relationships), and domain integrity (data types and value consistency).

- **SQL:** SQL is used for querying and manipulating the data stored in a relational database.

In Table 2-1, each row represents a student with a unique Student_id, their name is Student_Name, and the ID of the course in which they're enrolled is Course_id. The Course_id in Table 2-1 is a foreign key that connects Table 2-1 to Table 2-2.

In Table 2-2, each row represents a course with a unique Course_id and its name is Course_Name. The Course_id in this table is the primary key.

TABLE 2-1 Student table

Student_id	Student_Name	Course_id
1	John Doe	101
2	Jane Smith	102
3	Mary Johnson	103
4	James Brown	101

TABLE 2-2 Course table

Course_id	Course_Name
101	Mathematics
102	English
103	History

In the context of Azure, there are several services that are built on the relational model, such as Azure SQL Database and SQL Server on Azure VMs. These services allow you to work with relational data using SQL for managing and manipulating the relational data.

The relational concept is at the heart of most traditional database systems, and understanding it is key to becoming proficient in any database-related work, especially when working with Azure's data services.

> **NEED MORE REVIEW?** **RELATIONAL CONCEPTS**
>
> You can learn more about relational concept at *learn.microsoft.com/en-us/training/modules/ explore-relational-data-offerings/2-understand-relational-data.*

Describe normalization and how it is used

When you're designing a relational database, one of the key approaches you'll use is normalization. This process is all about organizing your data in a way that reduces redundancy and helps avoid any inconsistencies that could lead to confusion or errors.

You'll achieve normalization by dividing your data into multiple related tables, each one focused on specific data. These divisions are guided by rules known as *normal forms*. There are several normal forms, each with a specific set of rules. The main ones are first normal form, second normal form, third normal form, Boyce–Codd normal form, fourth normal form, and fifth normal form. Each successive normal form comes with stricter rules.

These are the benefits of normalization:

- **Reduces data redundancy:** By breaking down tables and eliminating duplicate data, normalization helps minimize redundancy.

- **Improves data consistency and integrity:** Normalization enforces rules that enhance data accuracy and reliability, reducing the likelihood of anomalies.

- **Simplifies query handling:** Well-organized data simplifies the process of querying, updating, and managing data.

- **Efficiently uses storage:** By reducing redundancy, normalization ensures efficient use of storage.

Normalization is conducted through a series of steps, or what we call *normal forms*:

1. **First normal form (1NF):** Ensures all columns in a table are atomic and each cell can contain only a single value. No repeating groups are allowed.

   Example: A Students table with a Subjects column storing comma-separated values violates 1NF. It should be divided into two tables: Students and Subjects.

2. **Second normal form (2NF):** Achieved when the table is in 1NF and all nonkey attributes are fully functionally dependent on the primary key.

   Example: A table with the columns StudentID, Subject, and Teacher, where Teacher depends on Subject, not on StudentID, violates 2NF. To achieve 2NF, divide the table to separate subjects and their teachers.

3. **Third normal form (3NF):** Achieved when the table is in 2NF and all the attributes are functionally dependent only on the primary key.

   Example: If a table contains StudentID, StudentAge, and StudentCity, and if StudentAge can be derived from StudentID, it should be moved to a separate table to satisfy 3NF.

4. **Boyce-Codd normal form (BCNF):** A stronger version of 3NF. A table is in BCNF if it is in 3NF, and for every functional dependency X → Y, X should be a superkey.

   Example: In a table with the columns StudentID, CourseID, and Instructor, if Instructor is dependent on CourseID and not on StudentID, the table should be split to satisfy BCNF.

5. **Fourth normal form (4NF):** Achieved when a table is in BCNF and does not have multi-valued dependencies.

   Example: A table with StudentID, Courses, and Hobbies, where Courses and Hobbies are independent multivalued facts about a student, violates 4NF. This should be divided into separate tables.

6. **Fifth normal form (5NF):** A table is in 5NF if it is in 4NF and there are no join dependencies that do not follow from the key constraints.

   Example: A complex scenario where a table involves a three-way relationship and breaking it down into smaller tables and then reconstructing it does not lose information.

Let's take a look at an example of normalizing the data in Table 2-3.

TABLE 2-3 Unnormalized table

Student_id	Student_Name	Course_ids	Course_Names
1	John Doe	101, 102	Math, English
2	Jane Smith	101	Math

After normalization, this data could be divided into three tables: Student, Course, and Enrollment (see Tables 2-4, 2-5, and 2-6).

TABLE 2-4 Normalized Student table

Student_id	Student_Name
1	John Doe
2	Jane Smith

TABLE 2-5 Normalized Course table

Course_id	Course_Name
101	Math
102	English

TABLE 2-6 Normalized Enrollment table

Student_id	Course_id
1	101
1	102
2	101

In this example, the Enrollment table establishes the relationship between the Student and Course tables. Now, if the course name changes, you need to update it in only one place, enhancing data consistency.

Challenges of normalization

While database normalization is a fundamental practice for optimizing database design, it brings with it a set of challenges that can impact the performance and manageability of your database systems. Understanding these challenges is crucial for database designers and administrators:

- **Complex queries:** Sometimes normalized tables lead to complex queries that might degrade performance.

- **Design complexity:** Achieving higher normal forms may result in a complex database design.

When to use normalization

Normalization should be used during the design phase of the database to ensure that the data is stored efficiently and the database can be maintained easily.

As you learn to work with databases in Azure and other platforms, understanding the principles and benefits of normalization will be invaluable. It's a tool that can help you create efficient, reliable, and manageable databases.

> **NEED MORE REVIEW?** **NORMALIZATION**
>
> You can learn more about normalization at *learn.microsoft.com/en-us/training/modules/ explore-relational-data-offerings/3-normalization.*

Identify common structured query language (SQL) statements

SQL is a standardized programming language that is used to manage and manipulate relational databases, as pictured in Figure 2-1. Developed in the 1970s at IBM by Donald D. Chamberlin and Raymond F. Boyce, SQL has been the de facto standard for interacting with relational databases for decades. Despite being more than a half-century old, SQL's power and ubiquity have ensured its relevance even in today's big data age.

FIGURE 2-1 Showing a SQL relational database

At its core, SQL allows you to create, manipulate, and query relational databases, which store data in structured tables. But beyond these basic capabilities, SQL is used in a variety of real-world scenarios. It powers business intelligence and drives decision-making in companies, and organizations can use it to gain insights from massive datasets. Whether you're a data analyst, a data scientist, a back-end developer, or even a machine learning engineer, understanding SQL is an invaluable skill.

However, you'll notice that different database systems support various SQL dialects. These dialects, while fundamentally the same, often come with their own set of proprietary extensions that are specific to a particular database system. These are some popular SQL dialects:

- **Transact-SQL (T-SQL):** This is Microsoft's proprietary extension of SQL, which includes a set of programmable functions and procedural programming. T-SQL is primarily used with Microsoft SQL Server.

- **PL/SQL:** This stands for Procedural Language/SQL, a dialect developed by Oracle. PL/SQL includes procedural language constructs, and it supports structured programming.

- **MySQL:** MySQL uses a dialect of SQL that is rich in functions, including string processing, date and time processing, and advanced features such as replication and partitioning.

- **PostgreSQL:** PostgreSQL supports a version of SQL that includes many features not available in other database systems, such as window functions and common table expressions.

Understanding these different dialects is valuable, especially when migrating from one database system to another for working with multiple database systems.

SQL statement types

SQL statements can be broadly classified into several types:

- Data Definition Language (DDL)
- Data Manipulation Language (DML)
- Data Control Language (DCL)
- Transaction Control Language (TCL)

DATA DEFINITION LANGUAGE

You'll use DDL statements to create, modify, or delete the structure of database objects. The common statements are CREATE, ALTER, and DROP, as shown in Table 2-7.

TABLE 2-7 DDL statements

Statement	Description
CREATE	Creates a new database, table, index, or stored procedure.
ALTER	Modifies an existing database object like a table. ALTER can be used to add, delete/drop, or modify columns in an existing table. It also can used to add and drop various constraints on an existing table.
DROP	Deletes an existing database, table, index, or view.
TRUNCATE	Marks the extents of a table for deallocation (empty for reuse). The result of this operation quickly removes all data from a table, typically bypassing a number of integrity-enforcing mechanisms intended to slow down data deletion.
RENAME	Renames an existing database object like a table.

Figure 2-2 shows an example of the DDL CREATE statement that has been used to create a new table named Student with two columns: StudentID with the data type INT (an integer, or whole number) and FirstName with the data type VARCHAR (VARCHAR stands for variable-length character data).

FIGURE 2-2 DDL CREATE statement

Figure 2-3 shows an ALTER statement that has been used to alter the Students table by adding a new column named Email with a data type of VARCHAR (255).

FIGURE 2-3 DDL ALTER statement

Figure 2-4 shows the DROP statement used to delete the Student table from the database.

FIGURE 2-4 DDL DROP statement

Figure 2-5 shows the TRUNCATE statement used to delete all the records from the Students table while keeping the table structure for future use.

FIGURE 2-5 DDL TRUNCATE statement

Figure 2-6 shows the RENAME statement used to rename the Statement table to Learners.

FIGURE 2-6 DDL RENAME statement

These DDL statements form the basis of structuring your data in a relational database. You'll frequently use these commands as you build and manage your databases, so be sure to get comfortable with their syntax and uses. Practice is key!

DATA MANIPULATION LANGUAGE

You'll use DML statements to insert, update, and delete data in a database. The common statements include INSERT, UPDATE, and DELETE, as shown in Table 2-8.

TABLE 2-8 DML statements

Statement	Description
INSERT	The INSERT statement adds new records into a table.
UPDATE	The UPDATE statement modifies existing records in a table.
DELETE	The DELETE statement removes existing records from a table.
SELECT	The SELECT statement fetches data from a database.
MERGE	The MERGE statement combines rows from two tables based on a related column between them. It's a combination of INSERT, UPDATE, and DELETE.

Figure 2-7 shows an example of a DML INSERT statement used to add a new record into the Students table. The new student has a StudentID of 1, a FirstName of John, and a LastName of Doe.

FIGURE 2-7 DML INSERT statement

Figure 2-8 shows the UPDATE statement used to update the Students table by changing the FirstName to Jane for the student with a StudentID of 1.

FIGURE 2-8 DML UPDATE statement

Figure 2-9 shows the DELETE statement used to remove records from the Students table where the StudentID is 1.

FIGURE 2-9 DML DELETE statement

Although technically part of the Data Query Language, SELECT is often considered part of DML as it is fundamental to manipulating data. The SELECT statement is used to fetch data from a database.

Figure 2-10 shows the SELECT statement fetching all the data from the Students table for the record where StudentID is 1.

FIGURE 2-10 DML SELECT statement

Figure 2-11 shows how to merge data from UpdatedStudents (based on StudentID) and insert new records from UpdatedStudents into Students.

```sql
MERGE INTO Students AS Target
USING
(SELECT StudentID, FirstName, LastName FROM UpdatedStudents) AS Source
ON Target.StudentID = Source.StudentID
WHEN MATCHED THEN
    UPDATE SET
        Target.FirstName = Source.FirstName,
        Target.LastName = Source.LastName
WHEN NOT MATCHED THEN
    INSERT (StudentID, FirstName, LastName)
    VALUES (Source.StudentID, Source.FirstName, Source.LastName);
```

FIGURE 2-11 DML MERGE statement

Mastering the DML statements is crucial for effective database operations and data management. Make sure to practice these commands with different tables and databases to thoroughly understand how they work.

DATA CONTROL LANGUAGE

You will use DCL to create roles, permissions, and referential integrity; it is also used to control access to databases by securing them. The common statements are GRANT, REVOKE, and DENY, as shown in Table 2-9.

TABLE 2-9 DCL statements

Statement	Description
GRANT	The GRANT statement gives permission to a user (or role) to perform certain operations, such as SELECT, INSERT, UPDATE, and DELETE on a certain object (like a table).
REVOKE	The REVOKE statement takes back permissions from a user (or role). This command is used when a user no longer needs access to an object or when their job's role changes.
DENY	The DENY statement denies permissions to a user (or role).

Figure 2-12 shows how to grant User1 permission to execute SELECT and INSERT operations on the Students table.

```sql
GRANT SELECT, INSERT ON Students TO User1;
```

FIGURE 2-12 DCL GRANT statement

Figure 2-13 shows how to revoke User1's permission to perform INSERT operations on the Students table.

FIGURE 2-13 DCL REVOKE statement

Figure 2-14 shows how to deny User1 the permission to perform DELETE operations on the Students table. Even if another rule grants User1 the DELETE permission, this DENY rule will override it.

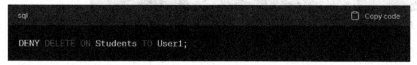

FIGURE 2-14 DCL DENY statement

Understanding these DCL statements is important for managing access control and ensuring data security in your database. Practice using these statements to gain a clear understanding of their impact on database operations. Make sure to always carefully consider the implications of granting, revoking, or denying permissions to maintain the integrity and security of your data.

TRANSACTION CONTROL LANGUAGE

TCL commands are used to manage transactions in the database. They include COMMIT, ROLLBACK, and SAVEPOINT, as shown in Table 2-10.

TABLE 2-10 TCL statements

Statement	Description
BEGIN TRANSACTION	The BEGIN TRANSACTION statement marks the starting point of an explicit, local SQL transaction.
COMMIT	The COMMIT statement saves all the changes made since the start of the transaction.
ROLLBACK	The ROLLBACK statement undoes all the changes made in the transaction.
SAVEPOINT	The SAVEPOINT command temporarily saves a transaction so that you can roll back to that point whenever necessary.

Figure 2-15 shows how you initialize a new transaction. Any SQL statements following this will be part of this transaction.

```sql
BEGIN TRANSACTION;
```

FIGURE 2-15 TCL BEGIN TRANSACTION statement

Figure 2-16 shows how to start a transaction, make an update to the Students table, and then commit the transaction. This means the update is saved and cannot be rolled back.

```sql
BEGIN TRANSACTION;
UPDATE Students SET FirstName = 'John' WHERE StudentID = 1;
COMMIT;
```

FIGURE 2-16 TCL COMMIT statement

Figure 2-17 shows a transaction started that is making an update to the Students table. However, you can decide to roll back the transaction, meaning the update to the Students table will not be saved and the data remains as it was before the transaction began.

```sql
BEGIN TRANSACTION;
UPDATE Students SET FirstName = 'John' WHERE StudentID = 1;
ROLLBACK;
```

FIGURE 2-17 DCL ROLLBACK statement

Figure 2-18 shows a transaction started that is making an update to the Students table, creating a savepoint, and making another update. Then, you decide to roll back the transaction to the savepoint. The first update will be saved, but the second update will not.

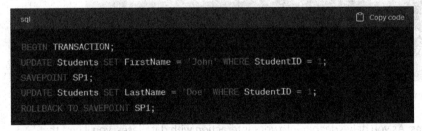

```sql
BEGIN TRANSACTION;
UPDATE Students SET FirstName = 'John' WHERE StudentID = 1;
SAVEPOINT SP1;
UPDATE Students SET LastName = 'Doe' WHERE StudentID = 1;
ROLLBACK TO SAVEPOINT SP1;
```

FIGURE 2-18 TCL SAVEPOINT statement

These TCL commands are crucial for maintaining the integrity of your data, especially in situations where you need to perform multiple related operations as a single atomic unit. If any of these operations fails, the TCL commands allow you to roll back the entire transaction, preventing your data from ending up in an inconsistent state.

NEED MORE REVIEW? **COMMON SQL STATEMENTS**

You can learn more about common SQL statements at *learn.microsoft.com/en-us/training/ modules/explore-relational-data-offerings/4-query-with-sql*.

Identify common database objects

Database objects are essential components that you will interact with while working with databases. These objects are utilized to store, manipulate, and retrieve the data housed within your database.

- **Tables:** *At the heart of any database are tables. They are the structure that holds the data. A table consists of rows (or records) and columns (or fields). Each column represents a category of data, and each row contains the actual data values, as shown in Table 2-11.*

TABLE 2-11 Table object

StudentID	FirstName	LastName
1	John	Coe
2	Jane	Smith
3	Mike	Johnson
4	Alice	Williams
5	Bob	Davis

- **Views:** A view is a virtual table based on the resultset of a SQL statement. They allow you to present the data in a different perspective from that of the base table, and they can hide complexity or secure sensitive data. Figure 2-19 shows how you would create a view called TopStudent that shows only those students with a GPA greater than 3.5.

```sql
CREATE VIEW TopStudents AS
SELECT FirstName, LastName
FROM Students
WHERE GPA > 3.5;
```

FIGURE 2-19 Simplifying data queries with a view to display top students

- **Indexes:** As you delve deeper into your interaction with databases, you'll find that indexes are fundamental to optimizing performance and enhancing the speed of data retrieval.

An index, in the context of a database, is similar to an index in a book. In a book, an index allows you to find information quickly without having to read every page. Similarly, a database index provides a quick lookup pathway to the data in a table.

Creating an index involves the CREATE INDEX statement. When you create an index on a table column, the database management system (DBMS) generates a data structure that allows it to find the data associated with the indexed columns more swiftly.

Let's look at an example. Say you frequently execute a query as shown in Figure 2-20 that searches students based on their last names in the Students table.

```sql
SELECT * FROM Students WHERE LastName = 'Smith';
```

FIGURE 2-20 The search query

To speed up this query, you can create an index on the LastName column, as shown in Figure 2-21.

```sql
CREATE INDEX idx_lastname ON Students (LastName);
```

FIGURE 2-21 Enhancing query efficiency with an index on the LastName column in the Students table

Now, the DBMS will use the idx_lastname index to find Smith rapidly, which can lead to significantly faster query performance.

However, while indexes are powerful, they should be used judiciously. Creating an index is not a trivial task for the DBMS. It takes time and consumes storage space. Moreover, every time a table's data changes (via an INSERT, UPDATE, or DELETE statement), the associated indexes also need to be updated. Thus, having too many indexes, especially on a table that frequently changes, can actually degrade the performance.

Therefore, a balanced approach is required when dealing with indexes. They should be created on columns that are frequently searched or used in the WHERE clause, JOIN operations, or sorting data (ORDER BY).

By implementing indexes in your database, you're well on your way to creating efficient, performance-tuned data retrieval options. This knowledge will greatly enhance your ability to effectively manage data in a relational database.

- **Stored procedures:** These are a group of SQL statements that form a logical unit and perform a particular task. Stored procedures can be used to encapsulate logic, enforce security, and increase performance.

In Figure 2-22 you could create a stored procedure to add a new student to the Students table.

```sql
                                                                    Copy code
CREATE PROCEDURE AddStudent @FirstName varchar(50), @LastName varchar(50)
AS
INSERT INTO Students (FirstName, LastName)
VALUES (@FirstName, @LastName);
```

FIGURE 2-22 Stored procedure

- **Triggers:** Triggers are special types of stored procedures that automatically execute when an event occurs in the database server. Triggers can help maintain the integrity of the data. You can create a trigger that automatically updates a LastModified field in the Students table whenever a record is updated, as shown in Figure 2-23.

```sql
                                                                    Copy code
CREATE TRIGGER UpdateLastModified ON Students
FOR UPDATE
AS
UPDATE Students
SET LastModified = GETDATE()
WHERE StudentID = Inserted.StudentID;
```

FIGURE 2-23 Trigger implementation to auto-update the LastModified timestamp in the Students table

By understanding and utilizing these objects, you can effectively manage your data and optimize your interactions with the database.

> **NEED MORE REVIEW?** **DATABASE OBJECTS**
>
> You can learn more about database objects at *learn.microsoft.com/en-us/training/modules/explore-relational-data-offerings/5-database-objects*.

Skill 2.2: Describe relational Azure data services

Having gained some familiarity with relational concepts and SQL, your next step is to explore relational data services within Azure. The Microsoft Azure cloud platform offers a suite of comprehensive and robust data services, catering to a wide array of relational database needs.

In this section, you will uncover the specifics of Azure's relational data offerings. You'll delve into the Azure SQL family of products, learning how each product fits into different scenarios based on the specific requirements. You'll explore the capabilities and uses of SQL Server on Azure Virtual Machines and how it offers flexibility in the migration process.

Furthermore, you will get acquainted with Azure database services for open-source database systems. Open-source databases have their unique features and community support, and

Azure provides first-class support for these systems, allowing you to leverage their capabilities in a cloud environment.

Upon completion of this section, you will have a good understanding of Azure's relational data services, empowering you to make informed decisions about which service best suits your data requirements. Let's begin this exciting journey into the world of Azure relational data services.

This skill covers how to:

- Describe the Azure SQL family of products including Azure SQL Database, Azure SQL, Azure Managed Instance, and SQL Server on Azure Virtual Machines
- Identify Azure database services for open-source database systems

---

Describe the Azure SQL family of products including Azure SQL Database, Azure SQL, Azure Managed Instance, and SQL Server on Azure Virtual Machines

Microsoft Azure provides a robust suite of SQL offerings, known collectively as the Azure SQL family. This portfolio of SQL-based services in Azure caters to a variety of needs, ranging from managing relational data to intelligent, cloud-native relational databases.

- **Azure SQL Database:** Azure SQL Database is a fully managed relational database service that provides the broadest SQL Server engine compatibility. It's an intelligent, scalable service that offers seamless integration with Azure services such as Azure Active Directory and Power BI. Azure SQL Database supports built-in intelligence that learns your unique database patterns and automatically tunes the database for improved performance and protection. You can use it to build data-driven applications and websites in your programming language of choice, without needing to manage any infrastructure.

- **Azure SQL Managed Instance:** Azure SQL Managed Instance provides the broadest SQL Server engine compatibility and native virtual network (VNet) support. It's a fully managed service, which allows you to migrate your SQL Server workloads to Azure with zero code changes. SQL Managed Instance is best for most migrations to the cloud as it provides a high degree of compatibility with the SQL Server programming surface area.

- **Azure SQL Server on Virtual Machines:** Azure SQL Server on Virtual Machines lets you run SQL Server inside a virtual machine in the cloud. This service is your best choice when you require full control over the SQL Server engine and the VM it runs on. It is suitable for migrating existing applications to the cloud with minimal changes or when you need SQL Server features that are not supported in Azure SQL Database or Azure SQL Managed Instance.

- **Azure Synapse Analytics:** Formerly SQL Data Warehouse, Azure Synapse Analytics is an analytics service that brings together big data and data warehousing. It gives you the freedom to query data on your terms, using serverless on-demand or provisioned resources.

- **Azure SQL Edge:** Azure SQL Edge is an optimized relational database engine geared toward Internet of Things (IoT) and edge computing scenarios. It offers a small footprint that can run a variety of devices from low-power edge devices to high-performance edge servers.

Azure SQL Edge provides the same SQL engine that powers SQL Server and Azure SQL, making it fully compatible with your existing SQL tools and skills. It supports data streaming through built-in stream analytics, machine learning scoring, and storage tiering.

What's even more exciting is that it allows data to be processed close to the source, minimizing latency and bandwidth usage. It can operate in connected, disconnected, and hybrid environments, synchronizing data with Azure SQL Database or Azure SQL Managed Instance whenever connectivity is available.

Figure 2-24 illustrates how Azure SQL Edge can fit into an IoT solution architecture.

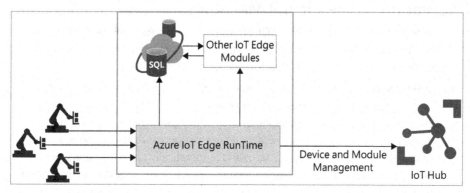

FIGURE 2-24 Azure SQL Edge

Comparing Azure SQL services

In the ever-evolving landscape of cloud services, Microsoft Azure presents a suite of SQL service offerings, each tailored to meet different operational and technological needs. From platform-as-a-service (PaaS) solutions designed for seamless management to infrastructure-as-a-service (IaaS) options that provide full control over your environment, Azure caters to a wide spectrum of data management scenarios. Table 2-12 compares the distinct characteristics, compatibilities, and use cases for each Azure SQL service offering, providing you with a clear overview to make informed decisions aligned with your business requirements.

TABLE 2-12 Comparative overview of Azure SQL services

	Azure SQL Database	Azure SQL Managed Instance	SQL Server on Azure VMS	Azure Synapse Analytics	Azure SQL Edge
Type of Cloud Service	PaaS	PaaS	IaaS	PaaS	IoT Edge solution
SQL Service Compatibility	High, but not 100%	Nearly 100%	100%	Partial	High, but optimized for edge computing
Architecture	Single or pooled databases	Instance scoped features	Full SQL Server instance	Data warehousing	Single database
Availability	Regional and zone redundant	Regional and zone redundant	Depending on VM setup	Regional and zone redundant	One edge device
Management	Fully managed	Fully managed	Self-managed	Fully managed	Self-managed
Use Cases	Modern cloud applications, microservices, and multitenant apps	Migrating on-premise workloads with minimal changes	Full control over SQL Server and VM and legacy applications; specific features not available in other offerings	Big data and data warehousing, analytics	IoT, edge computing, data streaming, disconnected environments

This table serves as a guide to help you discern which Azure SQL service is best suited for your specific data management needs, whether you're looking to modernize applications, manage big data, or extend SQL capabilities to the edge.

Azure SQL Database

Azure SQL Database is a fully managed relational database service provided by Microsoft Azure. It offers the broadest SQL Server engine compatibility and powers your cloud applications with a variety of built-in features such as intelligent performance tuning, scalability, high availability, and advanced security capabilities.

Azure SQL Database operates as a database as a service (DBaaS), meaning you don't have to worry about managing the underlying infrastructure. Instead, you can focus on optimizing your data and developing robust, data-driven applications.

USE CASES

Azure SQL Database, with its fully managed, scalable capabilities, is an exemplary choice for a range of contemporary application architectures. This managed database service is fine-tuned for the cloud environment, making it particularly well-suited for the following scenarios:

- **Modern cloud applications:** Azure SQL Database is an excellent choice for modern cloud applications because of its built-in intelligence and scalability features.

- **Microservices architectures:** Its ability to independently scale out database makes it suitable for microservices architecture where each microservice can have its dedicated database.

- **Multitenant applications:** If you're developing a SaaS application that needs to provide a separate, isolated database for each customer (multitenancy), Azure SQL Database is a great choice because of its isolated database capabilities.

BUSINESS BENEFITS

Azure SQL Database stands out in the realm of cloud services, offering a suite of benefits that underscore its value proposition for businesses seeking efficient, scalable, and secure database solutions. Embracing Azure SQL Database can lead to a more streamlined operational model with a focus on innovation and growth:

- **Lower total cost of ownership (TCO):** With Azure SQL Database, you don't need to purchase, set up, or manage any physical hardware, reducing your overall expenses. It also provides predictable billing and cost-efficiency with a pay-as-you-go model.

- **Scalability:** Azure SQL Database offers the ability to quickly scale resources up or down based on your needs. You can adjust compute and storage resources independently in seconds, ensuring you always have the resources you need without overpaying for excess capacity.

- **High availability and disaster recovery:** Azure SQL Database comes with built-in high availability, automated backups, and geo-replication capabilities. It ensures that your data is available and protected at all times, reducing the risk of data loss.

- **Advanced security:** Azure SQL Database provides a high level of security with features such as automated updates, threat detection, data encryption, and compliance with various international and industry-specific compliance standards.

- **Time savings:** Because Azure SQL Database is a fully managed service, you don't need to spend time on database administration tasks. Instead, you can focus on what truly matters: developing and optimizing your applications.

> **NEED MORE REVIEW?**   **AZURE SQL DATABASE**
>
> You can learn more about Azure SQL Database at *learn.microsoft.com/en-us/training/ modules/explore-provision-deploy-relational-database-offerings-azure/2-azure-sql.*

Azure SQL Managed Instance

Azure SQL Managed Instance is a powerful blend of the feature-rich capabilities of an on-premises SQL Server and the operational efficiency and PaaS benefits of Azure. It's a fully managed service that provides near-complete SQL Server compatibility and native virtual network support. This means you can migrate your on-premises SQL Server databases to Azure without altering the application code, making it an ideal solution for enterprises looking to move to the cloud while avoiding the complexity of refactoring their applications. Managed Instance comes with the luxury of automated patching, backups, and maintenance, plus built-in features such as threat detection and performance tuning. The service operates within Azure Virtual Network, which provides an additional layer of isolation and security, ensuring that your databases are not exposed to the public internet. For organizations with extensive use of SQL Server features such as SQL Agent jobs, Service Broker, or the Common Language Runtime (CLR), Azure SQL Managed Instance offers a seamless migration pathway with minimal downtime and maximum data retention.

SQL Server on Azure VMs

SQL Server on Azure VMs represents the IaaS side of Azure's database offerings, giving you full control over both the SQL Server instance and the virtual machine it runs on. This service is tailored for scenarios where specific SQL Server features or configurations are required, such as legacy applications that depend on a particular SQL Server version or need the database server within a Windows or Linux environment. With SQL Server on Azure VMs, you can replicate the on-premises experience in the cloud while also benefiting from Azure's built-in features such as automated backups, scalable storage, and robust networking capabilities. The choice of VM size, storage type, and SQL Server edition is in your hands, offering a high degree of customization. Additionally, you can take advantage of Azure's security and compliance offerings while maintaining the ability to implement your own security measures at the OS or database level. For workloads that require OS-level access or for companies that make use of extensive SQL Server administration, SQL Server on Azure VMs is an optimal choice.

Azure Synapse Analytics

Azure Synapse Analytics is a limitless analytics service that brings together big data and data warehousing. It offers a unique environment for processing large volumes of data in relational and non-relational formats. Synapse Analytics stands out with its ability to query data on-demand with serverless capabilities or to provision resources for more demanding workloads. It integrates deeply with other Azure services, providing a unified experience for ingesting, exploring, preparing, managing, and serving data for immediate BI and machine learning needs. Azure Synapse links with Azure Data Lake, which offers massive scale and secure data lake functionality. Moreover, it provides a unified experience for data prep, data management, data warehousing, big data, and AI tasks. The Synapse Analytics workspace brings together these components into a cohesive development environment that supports multiple programming languages and offers a code-free experience through a web-based interface.

Azure SQL Edge

Azure SQL Edge caters to the burgeoning realm of IoT and edge computing. It's designed to stretch the capabilities of SQL databases to edge devices, bringing data storage and processing capabilities closer to the source of data generation. SQL Edge offers a small-footprint database engine optimized for the edge, with built-in capabilities for streaming, storage, and AI-driven analytics. It supports a subset of the T-SQL language and integrates with Azure's IoT tools, thus providing a consistent programming model across your cloud and edge solutions. With Azure

SQL Edge, you can deploy data workloads on devices running on ARM and x64 architectures, ensuring flexibility across diverse hardware. It also brings robust security features, such as data encryption and support for private networks, ensuring that your edge data is well-protected. For scenarios that involve disconnected or semi-connected environments, intermittent cloud connectivity, or real-time analytics on the edge, Azure SQL Edge provides a streamlined and efficient solution.

Managed Instance and SQL Server on Azure Virtual Machines

As you navigate the transition from on-premises SQL Server environments to the cloud, you have two distinct pathways within the Azure ecosystem, each offering a unique blend of features and control levels: Azure SQL Managed Instance and SQL Server on Azure Virtual Machines.

Azure SQL Managed Instance is for those seeking to lift-and-shift their existing SQL workloads directly into the cloud without extensive reconfiguration. It is a bridge between the convenience of a fully managed PaaS and the familiarity of an on-premises SQL Server instance; therefore, it offers a swath of SQL features you've come to rely on, paired with the perks of a managed service.

SQL Server on Azure Virtual Machines caters to those demanding the utmost flexibility and control. This IaaS solution is akin to a canvas, providing the full SQL Server instance and the freedom to manage every aspect, from the operating system to the data platform, and mirroring the experience of an on-premises server but within Azure's scalable environment.

In this section, we will delve into the details of each service, dissecting their architectures, use cases, and the rich tapestry of features they offer. Whether your priority is seamless management or granular control, these Azure services will meet your business needs with precision and efficiency, propelling you into the future of cloud-based data management.

Managed Instance

Azure SQL Managed Instance is a deployment option of Azure SQL that bridges the gap between an on-premises SQL Server instance and the Azure cloud platform. It offers full compatibility with the SQL Server engine, enveloped in a fully managed PaaS offering and providing a "best-of-both-worlds" approach to database management.

This service provides a highly available, scalable, and secure SQL Server environment without the overhead of managing the underlying infrastructure. It does so by encapsulating the SQL Server instance in a fully managed Azure environment, thus offloading typical infrastructure responsibilities such as patching, backups, and high availability to Azure's automated services.

Azure SQL Managed Instance is built on an isolated and dedicated subnet within Azure Virtual Network, which allows for secure connectivity from your on-premises network to Azure via ExpressRoute or VPN Gateway. It's essentially a private cluster of resources that Azure provisions and manages for you. Figure 2-25 outlines the key benefits of Azure SQL Managed Instance.

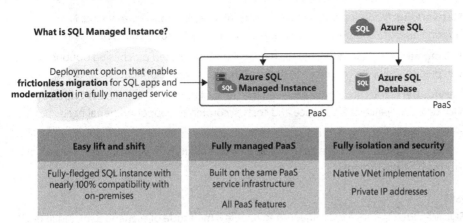

FIGURE 2-25 Azure SQL Managed Instance

ARCHITECTURAL COMPONENTS

To fully appreciate the robust capabilities of Azure SQL Managed Instance, it is crucial to understand its core architectural components. These components deliver a seamless and efficient database management experience:

- **Compute resources:** Provisioned as a scalable set of virtual machines running the SQL Server database engine, ensuring that compute capacity flexibly aligns with your workload demands.

- **Storage:** Automatically allocated from Azure's Premium Storage, guaranteeing high input/output operations per second (IOPS) and low latency for your data operations.

- **Automated backups:** Systematically stored in georedundant Azure Blob storage, providing resilient data recovery options and peace of mind.

- **Management service:** A built-in feature that oversees your instance, conducting automated updates and patches to maintain security and performance without manual intervention.

Each element plays a pivotal role in maintaining the service's high standards of performance, reliability, and convenience, setting the Azure SQL Managed Instance apart as a premier choice for database management in the cloud.

KEY FEATURES

The Azure SQL Managed Instance features cater to the diverse needs of modern-day database management, seamlessly bringing the SQL Server environment into the cloud. Here are its standout features:

- **SQL Server engine:** Managed Instance boasts nearly 100% compatibility with on-premises SQL Server, adeptly supporting a wide array of features required by current SQL Server workloads.

- **Networking:** Managed Instance seamlessly integrates within Azure Virtual Network, offering a secure and private network environment tailored to your SQL Server instance.
- **Pricing models:** Managed Instance has flexible vCore-based purchasing options so you can precisely allocate resources to fit the demands of your workload.
- **Service tiers:** You can choose between the General Purpose and Business Critical service tiers to balance performance and costs according to your operational needs.

These features underscore Azure SQL Managed Instance's commitment to providing a robust, versatile, and cost-effective database service that aligns with your business's scalability and performance requirements.

USE CASES

Azure SQL Managed Instance is engineered to handle a multitude of scenarios, shining in environments where specific SQL Server capabilities and considerations are paramount. Here are some of its more prominent use-cases scenarios:

- **Complex workloads:** Tailor-made for intricate SQL Server workloads, it embraces the full spectrum of SQL features, including SQL Agent, cross-database queries, and Common Language Runtime integration, to handle the most demanding tasks.
- **Compliance and security:** It is the go-to option when your applications are bound by stringent regulatory standards, offering a suite of advanced security measures and compliance controls.
- **Hybrid deployments:** For those navigating the hybrid landscape, Azure SQL Managed Instance ensures a smooth, secure connection between cloud-based resources and on-premises systems.

EXAMPLE SCENARIO

Consider a scenario where you are managing a SQL Server environment for a healthcare application that contains sensitive patient data. The application uses complex SQL Server functionalities, including SQL Agent jobs for scheduling tasks and the CLR for database-level computations. Compliance with health regulatory standards such as Health Insurance Portability and Accountability Act (HIPAA) is also a critical requirement.

To transition to Azure SQL Managed Instance, follow these steps:

1. Assess the compatibility of your SQL Server workloads using the Data Migration Assistant.
2. Plan the migration to Azure SQL Managed Instance considering the compute, storage, and performance needs.
3. Utilize the Azure Database Migration Service to migrate your on-premises SQL Server databases to Azure SQL Managed Instance with minimal downtime.
4. Configure a virtual network and ensure that network security groups are set up to allow traffic to and from your managed instance.

By choosing Azure SQL Managed Instance for this healthcare application, you ensure a seamless migration of your complex SQL workloads to a fully managed database service that complies with industry standards, thus maintaining the integrity and confidentiality of sensitive data.

Azure SQL Managed Instance is tailored for those who need the rich feature set of SQL Server coupled with the benefits of a managed, scalable, and secure cloud environment. It represents a strategic choice for businesses looking to modernize their database infrastructure while maintaining operational consistency.

> **NEED MORE REVIEW?** **AZURE SQL MANAGED INSTANCE**
>
> You can learn more about Azure SQL Managed Instance at learn.microsoft.com/en-us/ training/modules/explore-provision-deploy-relational-database-offerings-azure/2-azure-sql.

SQL Server on Azure Virtual Machines

In the realm of Azure cloud services, SQL Server on Azure Virtual Machines (VMs) is an offering that stands out for its familiar operational model and deep customization capabilities. This service embodies the IaaS model, providing you with the autonomy of managing SQL Server instances that are hosted on virtual machines in the Azure cloud.

SQL Server on Azure VMs presents a traditional SQL Server setup, but with the underlying hardware abstracted away. You're given the flexibility to choose the exact version and edition of SQL Server that aligns with your business needs, ranging from SQL Server 2008 to the most recent versions.

KEY ASPECTS OF SQL SERVER ON AZURE VMS

When setting up SQL Server on Azure Virtual Machines, you're equipped with an array of configurations to tailor your environment precisely to your workload's requirements. Here are the key aspects that highlight the adaptability and depth of SQL Server on Azure VMs:

- **Virtual machine choices:** Azure offers a diverse selection of VM series and sizes, ensuring you can find the perfect match for your SQL Server's operational demands, whether they lean toward general-purpose tasks, compute-intensive operations, or memory-heavy workloads.

- **Storage configuration:** With Azure's versatile storage solutions, you have the freedom to customize your storage setup to strike the right balance between performance needs and budget constraints, opting for high-speed SSDs or cost-effective HDDs as necessary.

- **Network integration:** The placement of your SQL Server VMs within Azure Virtual Network (VNet) provides secure, flexible networking options; you can seamlessly integrate it with your existing on-premises infrastructure, and you can configure public and private connectivity tailored to your security standards.

- **Licensing flexibility:** Azure caters to both new and existing SQL Server customers by offering a choice between bringing your own existing licenses to the cloud or utilizing the pay-as-you-go pricing model, which includes the SQL Server license, giving you financial and operational flexibility.

KEY FEATURES

SQL Server on Azure Virtual Machines is replete with features that not only bolster your data's resilience and security but also enhance performance and operational flexibility. The following are the key features that make SQL Server on Azure VMs a comprehensive solution for your database management needs:

- **Automated backup:** Azure streamlines the data protection process with automated backup solutions that you can tailor to your specific recovery point objectives, ensuring that both system and user-initiated backups are within easy reach for point-in-time restores.

- **High availability and disaster recovery:** Utilize Azure's expansive infrastructure to architect high availability solutions, such as Always On availability groups, and tap into Azure Site Recovery for robust disaster recovery plans, keeping your systems reliable and resilient.

- **Security enhancements:** While Azure inherently secures your VMs, you retain the option to further bolster your defenses, implementing granular security measures at the SQL Server and OS levels to safeguard your data comprehensively.

- **Performance optimization:** Azure grants you the tools for advanced monitoring and automatic tuning, empowering you to refine the performance of your SQL Server VMs for peak efficiency tailored to your unique workload demands.

- **Hybrid flexibility:** Embrace the versatility of Azure's hybrid capabilities to seamlessly meld your on-premises infrastructure with the cloud, creating a harmonious, unified platform for managing your databases across environments.

USE CASES

SQL Server on Azure Virtual Machines is not just a service but a versatile solution, adept at addressing a wide range of operational scenarios that demand specific SQL Server functionalities and configurations. Here's how this service can be instrumental across various use cases:

- **Legacy system support:** Azure VMs are a sanctuary for your older SQL Server versions that require a familiar environment, providing a cloud-based haven for your legacy systems and ensuring uninterrupted service without the need for immediate upgrades.

- **Customized solutions:** When your workloads demand unique SQL Server configurations or the integration of specialized features, such as third-party plugins or specific compatibility settings, Azure VMs stand ready to offer the exact level of control and customization you need.

- **Development and testing:** Offering the agility to swiftly spin up or wind down environments, Azure VMs are perfectly suited for development and testing, providing an environment that closely mirrors your production settings for accurate testing and development.

EXAMPLE SCENARIO

Let's say you're managing a data warehousing solution built on SQL Server 2016 with significant reliance on SQL Server Analysis Services (SSAS). Here's how you could implement this on Azure VMs:

1. Select and provision an appropriate VM size from the Azure portal, considering the compute, memory, and I/O requirements of your SSAS workloads.

2. Attach premium solid-state drive (SSD) storage to ensure quick data processing and set up automated backups with geo-redundancy.

3. Configure Azure VNet for secure access and establish a virtual private network (VPN) connection to your on-premises network.

4. Install SQL Server 2016 and configure SSAS, mirroring your on-premises setup.

5. Optimize the VM for performance, adjusting settings based on the monitoring insights provided by Azure.

SQL Server on Azure VMs is the quintessential choice for data professionals who require the comprehensive capabilities of SQL Server combined with the scalability, security, and reliability of Azure's infrastructure. Whether your workload is heavy on data processing or you need specific SQL Server features, Azure VMs provide a robust environment to meet and adapt to your evolving business needs.

> **NEED MORE REVIEW?** **SQL SERVER ON AZURE VIRTUAL MACHINES**
>
> You can learn more about SQL Server on Azure Virtual Machines at *learn.microsoft.com/en-us/ training/modules/explore-provision-deploy-relational-database-offerings-azure/2-azure-sql*.

Identify Azure database services for open-source database systems

Now let's expand your knowledge to encompass Azure's offerings in the realm of open-source databases. You'll delve into the various services Azure provides to accommodate the vast ecosystem of open-source database systems such as MySQL, PostgreSQL, and Maria DB. These databases have been widely adopted in industries and enterprises worldwide for their robustness, flexibility, and compatibility with various data models and languages. Azure's managed services for these databases provide a scalable, secure, and fully managed environment that retains all the benefits of open-source solutions while freeing you from the administrative and maintenance tasks. By the end of this section, you'll be well-versed in identifying and describing the key features, advantages, and use cases of Azure's database services for these open-source systems.

What are MySQL, MariaDB, and PostgreSQL?

My SQL, MariaDB, and PostgreSQL are all popular open-source relational database management systems (RDBMSs). Each has unique features and benefits that make them suitable for different applications and use cases.

- **MySQL:** MySQL is a widely used open-source RDBMS. It is known for its speed, reliability, and ease of use. MySQL is often used in web applications and online publishing and is a central component of the popular LAMP open-source web application software stack (Linux, Apache, MySQL, PHP/Python/Perl).

- **MariaDB:** MariaDB is a fork of MySQL created by the original developers of MySQL, and it's intended to remain open-source. MariaDB is designed to be highly compatible with MySQL, meaning that, in most cases, data and code can be switched seamlessly between the two. MariaDB includes more storage engines than MySQL, and it includes several features not found in MySQL.

- **PostgreSQL:** PostgreSQL is a powerful, open-source object-relational database system. It supports both SQL (relational) and JSON (non-relational) querying. It's highly extensible and can be customized via functions and stored procedures. PostgreSQL is renowned for its performance, advanced features, and standards compliance.

While all three systems can manage relational data, they each have unique advantages. MySQL is known for its speed and efficiency, MariaDB offers rich features and compatibility with MySQL, and PostgreSQL is known for its standards compliance and versatility. All three are supported by Azure, allowing you to leverage these benefits in a fully managed cloud environment.

Azure Database for MySQL

Azure Database for MySQL is a relational database service in the Microsoft cloud based on MySQL Community Edition (available version 5.6/5.7/8.0). As a fully managed service, it allows developers to focus more on developing applications and less on managing infrastructure.

- **Fully managed:** This service is fully managed by Microsoft. What does that mean for you? It means that common maintenance operations such as patching, backups, and handling failovers are automated. These features help save time and reduce the complexity of administrative tasks, freeing you to focus on what matters: developing your applications and improving functionality.

- **Performance and scalability:** Performance is a crucial aspect of any application. With Azure Database for MySQL, you have various options to match your performance requirements. Azure offers a range of compute sizes, so you can select the right amount of compute power you need. It allows you to independently scale compute and storage. This means you can adjust the compute power and storage space to match the demand of your application. This independent scaling is especially helpful as it provides flexibility and helps to manage costs.

- **Security and compliance:** Security and compliance are top priorities for any business. Azure Database for MySQL integrates well with Azure's advanced security and compliance services. It supports Azure Active Directory authentication so that identities can be managed in one central location. It also provides encryption at rest and in transit, adding a layer of protection to your data.

In addition, Azure offers a comprehensive set of compliance offerings. Whether you are dealing with general data protection regulations or industry-specific ones, Azure has you covered.

- **Developer productivity:** Azure Database for MySQL integrates seamlessly with popular open-source applications and Azure services. This makes it a natural choice if you are developing apps with Azure App Service, building microservices with Azure Kubernetes Services, or running analytics with Power BI.

- **Data protection:** Data is the heart of your business. To protect it, Azure Database for MySQL offers automatic backups, which are stored in geo-redundant storage. This allows you to restore your database to any point within the backup retention period. Additionally, the service provides the option to increase your retention period and to use long-term backup retention.

- **Global availability and industry-leading service-level agreements (SLAs):** With Azure's global footprint, you can run your applications closer to your customers. And with industry-leading SLAs, you can have peace of mind knowing your app will run smoothly and reliably.

In the following section, we will delve deeper into the business benefits and use cases of Azure Database for MySQL.

BUSINESS BENEFITS

When it comes to managing relational databases in the cloud, Azure Database for MySQL stands out as a service that not only streamlines operations but also scales seamlessly and ensures robust security. Here are some of the core benefits that this managed database service offers:

- **Reduce administrative overhead:** By using a fully managed service such as Azure Database for MySQL, you can focus on the application development side of things rather than managing the database infrastructure. Capabilities such as automatic patching, backup, and recovery are taken care of for you.

- **Scalability on demand:** With the scalable nature of Azure Database for MySQL, you can dynamically adjust resources to meet the changing demands of your application. This flexibility allows you to efficiently manage your workloads without substantial manual invention.

- **Robust security:** Security is paramount when dealing with databases. Azure Database for MySQL incorporates various security measures such as Azure AD authentication, firewall rules, and data encryption at rest and during transit via SSL connections. This added layer of security helps protect your data and reduce the risk of breaches.

- **Compliance:** Azure is compliant with a broad set of international and industry-specific regulatory standards. This includes General Data Protection Regulation (GDPR), International Organization for Standardization (ISO) 27001, Health Insurance Portability and Accountability Act (HIPAA), Service Organization Control (SOC), and others, which can be critical for businesses dealing with sensitive data.

These benefits highlight how Azure Database for MySQL can be a strategic asset for your business, ensuring operational efficiency, scalability, security, and compliance, all within a managed cloud service.

USE CASES

Azure Database for MySQL is a versatile cloud database service that caters to a wide array of applications and scenarios, capitalizing on its managed nature and the scalability of Azure. Let's explore how this service aligns with various use cases:

- **Web and mobile applications:** Azure Database for MySQL is ideal for running web and mobile applications. It supports popular languages and frameworks, which allows developers to continue using the tools they're familiar with while benefiting from Azure's managed service.

- **Content management systems (CMSs):** Many popular content management systems such as WordPress, Joomla, and Drupal use MySQL as their back-end database. Azure Database for MySQL provides a scalable, reliable, and secure platform for hosting these systems.

- **E-commerce platforms:** E-commerce platforms such as WooCommerce and Magento can benefit from Azure Database for MySQL's scalability and reliability, particularly during peak demand periods.

- **Data warehousing:** With Azure Database for MySQL, you can store and analyze large volumes of data, making it a suitable option for data warehousing use cases. It also integrates with Azure's analytics and AI services, providing comprehensive tools for your data warehousing needs.

- **Mitigation:** If you're running on-premises MySQL databases and planning a migration to the cloud, Azure Database for MySQL could be a prime choice. It offers minimal downtime during migration and compatibility with your existing MySQL applications.

Remember, the specific benefits and use cases for your organization may vary based on your particular situation and requirements. It's essential to carefully evaluate these aspects when deciding whether Azure Database for MySQL is right for you.

Azure Database for MariaDB

Azure Database for MariaDB is a fully managed relational database service provided by Microsoft Azure based on the open-source MariaDB Server engine. It's part of Azure's suite of fully managed database services, designed to save you time and resources in managing your database and allowing you to focus on your application development. Azure Database for

MariaDB offers automated patching, backups, and monitoring, making your database maintenance tasks easier.

MariaDB is a popular open-source database, developed by the original creators of MySQL. It is designed to remain free and open-source software under the GNU GPL. It's largely compatible with MySQL, while offering more robust, scalable, and reliable SQL server capabilities. MariaDB is developed with a focus on performance and stability, and it includes a rich set of features such as advanced query optimization and a variety of storage engines.

- **Fully managed service:** Azure Database for MariaDB is a fully managed database service, meaning that Microsoft handles much of the heavy lifting associated with database management. This includes server maintenance, failover, and disaster recovery capabilities. This way, you can focus on designing and coding your applications rather than dealing with the intricacies of database administration.

- **Security and compliance:** Azure Database for MariaDB integrates with Azure's advanced security and compliance services. It includes protection capabilities such as Advanced Threat Protection, which can detect anomalous activities indicating unusual and potentially harmful attempts to access or exploit your database. You can also manage and monitor all activity within your database using Azure Monitor and Azure Log Analytics.

- **Integration with Azure Services:** This database service also integrates well with other Azure services, allowing you to build comprehensive, cloud-based applications. You can integrate your database with Azure App Service for creating web and mobile apps, with Azure Functions for serverless computing, or with Azure Logic Apps for building automated workflows.

Now let's dive deeper inro the business benefits and use cases of Azure Database for MariaDB.

BUSINESS BENEFITS

Azure Database for MariaDB streamlines the management of your database systems, allowing you to focus on what matters most: developing applications that drive your business forward. This managed service combines the ease of operation with high availability, security, and seamless integration with other Azure services:

- **Managed service:** As a fully managed service, Azure Database for MariaDB takes away the burdens of typical database administration tasks, such as updates, backups, and scaling, allowing you to focus more on application development.

- **Scalability:** The service allows you to scale compute and storage independently, giving you the flexibility to adjust resources based on your application's needs.

- **High availability:** With built-in high availability and fault tolerance, you don't have to worry about unplanned downtimes affecting your applications.

- **Security:** Azure Database for MariaDB provides robust security measures, including Azure Active Directory integration, firewall protection, SSL encryption, and threat detection, ensuring your data is well protected.

- **Integration:** It seamlessly integrates with other Azure services, making it easier for you to create comprehensive cloud-based solutions.

Azure Database for MariaDB is designed to provide a worry-free database service that supports the continuity, security, and scalability of your applications with the added benefits of Azure's cloud infrastructure.

USE CASES

Azure Database for MariaDB is tailored to accommodate a diverse range of applications, capitalizing on its compatibility and integration within the Azure ecosystem. This managed database service is particularly well-suited for a variety of use cases that demand reliability, performance, and scalability:

- **Web and mobile applications:** Given its compatibility with popular programming languages and frameworks, Azure Database for MariaDB is ideal for building and running web and mobile applications.

- **CMS platforms:** The service can power various content management systems (CMSs), such as WordPress, Joomla, or Drupal, offering a secure, scalable, and reliable database platform.

- **E-commerce platforms:** E-commerce platforms, such as Magento or WooCommerce, can greatly benefit from Azure Database for MariaDB's scalability, especially during high-demand periods.

- **Data warehousing:** For organizations looking to analyze large volumes of data, Azure Database for MariaDB, combined with Azure's analytic services, can create a robust data warehousing solution.

- **Data migration:** If you're looking to migrate your on-premises MariaDB to the cloud, Azure Database for MariaDB provides a straightforward path with minimal downtime, letting you enjoy the benefits of a cloud-based database sooner.

Remember, your specific needs and requirements will dictate the benefits you derive and the use cases relevant to you. Therefore, it's important to understand these factors when choosing Azure Database for MariaDB.

Azure Database for PostgreSQL

Azure Database for PostgreSQL is an enterprise-ready, fully managed database service provided by Microsoft Azure. It's based on the popular open-source PostgreSQL database, designed to handle a broad range of applications from small single-machine applications to large internet-facing applications with numerous concurrent users.

PostgreSQL is widely respected for its robustness, functionality, and performance capabilities. It supports a wide range of built-in and user-defined data types, out-of-the-box full-text search, and numerous extensions, including the popular PostGIS for geospatial analysis.

- **Managed services:** When you use Azure Database for PostgreSQL, you're offloading your database administration tasks to Azure. Microsoft takes care of patching, updates, backups, and failure detection/recovery, allowing you to focus on your application and business logic. This SLA offers high availability and guarantees no data loss if a failure occurs.

- **Performance and scalability:** The service provides built-in high performance and scalability, supporting up to 64 TB of storage and 20,000 IOPS. You can easily scale your compute resources up or down in response to changes in workload demands.

- **Security and compliance:** Azure Database for PostgreSQL provides advanced security and compliance, with features such as Azure Active Directory integration for identity and access management, firewall rules to restrict network access to your database, SSL connections for secure data transfer, and compliance with various standards such as ISO/IEC 27001 and HIPAA.

- **Development productivity:** As part of the Azure ecosystem, Azure Database for PostgreSQL provides integration with various Azure services and developer tools. These include Azure DevOps for continuous integration/continuous deployment (CI/CD), Visual Studio Code extension for PostgreSQL, and Azure Data Studio for a rich query editing experience.

With these features, Azure Database for PostgreSQL is equipped to serve as the backbone for a variety of applications, whether it's for a small project or a large enterprise-level application. However, knowing the capabilities and features is only part of the story. Let's now delve into the business benefits and use cases that this service offers.

BUSINESS BENEFITS

Azure Database for PostgreSQL streamlines the operation and management of database services, allowing you to channel your efforts toward innovation and growth. Here's how this managed service can transform your database management experience:

- **Managed service:** With Azure Database for PostgreSQL, you can delegate the tedious task of database administration, such as updates, backups, and scaling, to Azure, leaving you to focus more on your application development.

- **Scalability:** The service offers you the flexibility to adjust compute and storage resources based on your application's needs, ensuring that your database capacity grows with your application.

- **High availability:** Azure Database for PostgreSQL comes with built-in high availability, protecting your applications from unplanned downtime.

- **Security:** The services provide robust security features such as Azure Active Directory integration, firewall rules, SSL enforcement, and threat detection, which help to ensure the safety and privacy of your data.

- **Developer productivity:** Integrating with various Azure services and developer tools, Azure Database for PostgreSQL helps developers remain productive and efficient.

With Azure Database for PostgreSQL, you're not just investing in a database service; you're helping your business leverage a secure, scalable, and high-performing data management platform that aligns with the dynamic needs of modern applications.

USE CASES

Azure Database for PostgreSQL is a fully managed database service that shines across several use cases because of its versatility, performance, and feature set. Here are some scenarios where Azure Database for PostgreSQL can be particularly advantageous:

- **Web and mobile applications:** Azure Database for PostgreSQL is excellent for running responsive web and mobile applications, thanks to its performance, scalability, and support for various features and datatypes.

- **Data analytics:** For those in the field of data analytics, this service is a compelling option because of its compatibility with various data visualization tools and analytics platforms.

- **Geospatial application:** PostgreSQL's advanced support for spatial data and operations means that Azure Database for PostgreSQL can serve as a backbone of geospatial application.

- **Migration:** If you're thinking of migrating your on-premises PostgreSQL database to the cloud, this service offers a seamless and secure migration path.

The benefits and use cases of Azure Database for PostgreSQL can vary according to your specific needs and requirements. Understanding these aspects can help you make the most out of this service.

EXAM TIP

For the DP-900 exam, it's important to understand the difference between Azure's various SQL offerings, including Azure SQL Database, Azure SQL Managed Instance, and SQL Server on Azure Virtual Machines.

Remember:

- Azure SQL Database is a fully managed PaaS with built-in intelligence. It is best for new applications that need scalability and minimal management.

- Azure SQL Managed Instance is also a fully managed PaaS, but it provides full SQL Server compatibility. It is best for migrating on-premises SQL Server applications to the cloud with minimal changes.

- SQL Server on Azure Virtual Machines is IaaS where you have control over both the OS and SQL Server instance. It is best for applications requiring complete control of the OS and SQL Server instance.

In addition, be sure you're familiar with the fundamentals of relational data, including normalization, Structured Query Language, and basic database objects such as tables, views, and indexes.Focus on understanding concepts and use cases rather than memorizing specifics. Always consider the business requirements and trade-offs when choosing a solution.

It might also be useful to get some hands-on experience with Azure SQL services through the Azure portal to better understand their functionalities and use cases.

Chapter summary

- Explored the concept of relational data and how it forms the basis of most database structures. Discussed how tables with rows and columns are used to model entities and relationships in a relational database.

- Dove into the concept of normalization and its uses in relational databases. Discussed the purpose of normalization to reduce data redundancy and improve data integrity.

- Gained insight into Structured Query Language (SQL), including its history, uses, and importance as the standard language for managing and manipulating relational databases.

- Examined the four types of SQL statements: Data Definition Language (DDL), Data Manipulation Language (DML), Data Control Language (DCL), and Transaction Control Language (TCL). Provided examples and explanations for each.

- Discussed common database objects such as tables, views, indexes, stored procedures, and triggers. Offered examples of how these objects work with a database.

- Delved into the Azure SQL family of products, including Azure SQL Database, Azure SQL Managed Instance, and SQL Server on Azure Virtual Machines. Discussed the use cases and business benefits for each.

- Compared Azure SQL services in terms of cloud service type, SQL Server compatibility, architecture, availability, management, and use cases.

- Offered a closer look at specific Azure SQL services including Azure SQL Managed Instance and Azure SQL Database. Reviewed their use cases and business benefits.

- Explored SQL Server on Azure Virtual Machines, with an emphasis on use cases and business benefits, and provided an example of how to set it up.

- Finally, gave a brief overview of Azure Database Services for open-source database systems, highlighting Azure's support for a range of open-source relational database systems.

Thought experiment

Navigating the cloud can be a complex task with various services and configurations to consider. To ensure you're well-prepared to make informed decisions about deploying Azure SQL services, let's engage in a thought experiment. These scenarios will test your understanding of Azure's database offerings, focusing on real-world applications and the technical considerations that accompany them. From the nuances of database management to the intricacies of compliance and performance optimization, these questions will challenge you to apply your knowledge to determine the best Azure SQL services for specific use cases. Reflect on the scenarios presented and select the options that best align with the requirements; then delve into the explanations provided to solidify your understanding of Azure's diverse and powerful database solutions.

1. You are planning to migrate an existing on-premises SQL Server database to Azure and want to ensure full SQL Server feature compatibility with minimal changes. Which service should you choose?

   A. Azure SQL Database

   B. Azure SQL Managed Instance

   C. SQL Server on Azure VMs

   D. Azure Synapse Analytics

2. An application requires a relational database with high throughput and low latency. Which Azure storage option would be most appropriate?

   A. Azure Blob storage

   B. Azure Table storage

   C. Azure Premium SSD

   D. Azure Standard HDD

3. Which Azure SQL service is fully managed and best suited for applications that require a single or pooled database with less complexity?

   A. Azure SQL Managed Instance

   B. SQL Server on Azure VMs

   C. Azure Synapse Analytics

   D. Azure SQL Database

4. If you need to create a complex data warehousing solution that involves big data and analytics, which Azure service is the most appropriate?

   A. Azure SQL Database

   B. Azure SQL Managed Instance

   C. SQL Server on Azure VMs

   D. Azure Synapse Analytics

5. When would you consider using SQL Server on Azure VMs over other Azure SQL offerings?

   A. When you need a fully managed database

   B. When you need the most cost-effective solution

   C. When you require full control over the SQL Server and the operating system

   D. When you want to use serverless computing

6. Your company has a web application that requires a database with the ability to scale resources automatically in response to varying loads. Which feature should you look for in an Azure SQL service?

   A. Automated backups

   B. High availability

   C. on Demand

   D. Compliance certifications

7. A business requires a relational database service that includes built-in intelligence to optimize performance and protect against threats. Which Azure SQL service includes these features?

   A. Azure SQL Database

   B. Azure SQL Managed Instance

   C. SQL Server on Azure VMs

   D. Azure Synapse Analytics

8. A developer is looking for a relational database service that allows the use of Azure Active Directory for authentication purposes. Which Azure SQL service should they use?

   A. Azure SQL Database

   B. Azure SQL Managed Instance

   C. SQL Server on Azure VMs

   D. All of the above

9. You are tasked with setting up a database for an IoT application that needs to process data close to the source in real time. Which Azure service is optimized for such edge computing scenarios?

   A. Azure SQL Database

   B. Azure SQL Managed Instance

   C. SQL Server on Azure VMs

   D. Azure SQL Edge

10. You need to implement a robust database solution for a mission-critical application that requires minimal downtime and guarantees data consistency across several geographic regions. Which Azure SQL service feature would best meet these requirements?

    A. Active geo-replication in Azure SQL Database

    B. Auto-failover groups in Azure SQL Managed Instance

    C. Always On availability groups in SQL Server on Azure VMs

    D. Geo-redundant storage in Azure Synapse Analytics

11. Your organization requires a SQL solution on Azure that must be compatible with the Linux operating systems and requires direct OS-level access for custom software installations. Which Azure SQL service should you choose?

    A. Azure SQL Database

    B. Azure SQL Managed Instance

    C. SQL Server on Azure VMs

    D. Azure Synapse Analytics

12. If you need to perform real-time analytics on a stream of data from sensors deployed globally and require low-latency read and write operations, which Azure SQL service would best fit your needs?

    A. Azure SQL Database

    B. Azure SQL Managed Instance

    C. SQL Server on Azure VMs

    D. Azure SQL Edge

13. You are developing a multitenant SaaS application that requires database isolation for each tenant but wants to manage all databases centrally. Which Azure SQL service feature would you leverage?

    A. Elastic pools in Azure SQL Database

    B. Managed instances in Azure SQL Managed Instance

    C. Individual databases in SQL Server on Azure VMs

    D. Workspaces in Azure Synapse Analytics

14. A company needs to ensure their database solution complies with the General Data Protection Regulation (GDPR). Which of the following Azure SQL services inherently provides compliance support for GDPR?

    A. Azure SQL Database

    B. Azure SQL Managed Instance

    C. SQL Server on Azure VMs

    D. All of the above

15. Your organization requires a database solution that allows for complex analytical queries and reporting on large historical datasets. Which Azure SQL service is specifically optimized for this type of workload?

    A. Azure SQL Database

    B. Azure SQL Managed Instance

    C. SQL Server on Azure VMs

    D. Azure Synapse Analytics

Thought experiment answers

This section contains the answers to the thought experiment. Each answer explains why the answer choice is correct.

1. **B** Azure SQL Managed Instance

   Explanation: Azure SQL Managed Instance is specifically designed for complex enterprise environments that require broad SQL Server feature compatibility. It supports SQL Server features like SQL Agent, Service Broker, and CLR integration, making it the preferred choice for businesses looking to migrate their on-premises SQL Server databases to the cloud with the least amount of application and database changes. Additionally, it offers the managed PaaS benefits such as automated patching and version updates, integrated VNet connectivity, and native support for database migration tools.

2. **C** Azure Premium SSD

   Explanation: Azure Premium SSDs are optimized for enterprise-grade storage performance and are the recommended choice for I/O-intensive workloads such as relational databases that require consistent low-latency and high IOPS. They are built on solid-state drives, which provide significantly faster read and write times compared to traditional spinning hard disks and are ideal for transactional database applications where rapid data access is crucial.

3. **D** Azure SQL Database

   Explanation: Azure SQL Database is engineered as a managed database service that simplifies deployment, scaling, and management of applications. It is especially suited for modern cloud applications that need to quickly adapt to changing demands, offering managed resources that can automatically scale. Its architecture supports both single databases for isolated workloads and elastic pools to efficiently manage the performance of multiple databases that have variable and unpredictable usage demands.

4. **D** Azure Synapse Analytics

   Explanation: Azure Synapse Analytics is Azure's analytics service that combines big data and data warehousing capabilities, providing a comprehensive service for complex analytics projects. It allows the use of either on-demand queries for serverless data exploration or provisioned resources for large-scale data transformation processes. Synapse Analytics integrates with a vast array of Azure services, including Power BI and Azure Machine Learning, for end-to-end analytics solutions, making it ideal for data warehousing and big data solutions.

5. **C** When you require full control over the SQL Server and the operating system

   Explanation: SQL Server on Azure VMs gives you the most granular level of control over the database and operating system environment, essentially mirroring the on-premises SQL Server experience in the cloud. This option is essential for workloads that rely on specific SQL Server features that are not yet available in managed instances, require specific OS-level customizations, or when you need to use particular third-party software that must be installed on the same machine as SQL Server.

6. **C** Scalability on demand

Explanation: Scalability on demand is a feature that's especially relevant in cloud-based database services like Azure SQL Database and Azure SQL Managed Instance, because you can automatically adjust the compute and storage resources in response to your application's performance requirements. This capability ensures that your database service remains responsive during peak usage periods and is cost-effective during times of low demand, all without the need for manual intervention.

7. **B** Azure SQL Managed Instance

Explanation: Azure SQL Managed Instance provides a balance between a managed service and a customizable SQL Server environment. It has built-in intelligent features that automate performance tuning based on the workload patterns it observes, and it includes advanced threat protection capabilities to automatically identify and mitigate potential security threats, which are essential for maintaining data security and performance in cloud environments.

8. **D** All of the above

Explanation: Azure Active Directory (AAD) integration for authentication is a security feature supported across Azure's SQL services, including Azure SQL Database, Azure SQL Managed Instance, and SQL Server on Azure VMs. This integration centralizes the management of users and groups, streamlines permission management, and provides the ability to apply conditional access policies, resulting in enhanced security and simplified administration.

9. **D** Azure SQL Edge

Explanation: Azure SQL Edge is optimized for edge computing scenarios, providing a database service that can be run on devices at the edge of the network, close to the data sources. It is designed for small-footprint environments and includes features for streaming, time-series, and AI-powered analytics, all crucial for real-time processing in Internet of Things (IoT) and edge computing applications. This makes it the optimal choice for scenarios that require processing data near its source to reduce latency and quickly act on insights derived from that data.

10. **A** Active geo-replication in Azure SQL Database

Explanation: Active geo-replication in Azure SQL Database is a feature designed for applications requiring high availability and geographic redundancy. It allows you to create readable secondary replicas of your database in different regions, which can be used for load balancing read-only workloads and for failover in case of regional outages, ensuring minimal downtime. This service maintains data consistency with up to a five-second recovery point objective (RPO), making it suitable for mission-critical applications that cannot afford significant data loss or downtime. Auto-failover groups and Always On availability groups also provide high availability solutions but are scoped differently within Azure's services, and geo-redundant storage in Azure Synapse Analytics focuses on data warehousing scenarios rather than active regional failover.

11. **C** SQL Server on Azure VMs

    Explanation: SQL Server on Azure VMs is the optimal choice when you need direct access to the operating system to install custom software or when you need to run SQL Server on a Linux environment. This service allows you full control over the VM, including the choice of the operating system, providing the flexibility required for such specific requirements.

12. **D** Azure SQL Edge

    Explanation: Azure SQL Edge is designed to operate in edge computing environments and IoT scenarios, where processing data closer to the source is critical. It provides the capabilities required for streaming data and real-time analytics, making it ideal for handling data from globally deployed sensors with the need for low-latency operations.

13. **A** Elastic pools in Azure SQL Database

    Explanation: Elastic pools in Azure SQL Database are designed for multitenant SaaS applications that need to manage a collection of databases with varying and unpredictable usage demands. This feature allows you to allocate performance resources to a pool that can be shared by multiple databases, offering both isolation and efficient resource utilization.

14. **D** All of the above

    Explanation: All Azure SQL services offer built-in compliance features that support GDPR, among other regulatory standards. Microsoft ensures that its cloud services are compliant with GDPR, providing features such as data protection, privacy, and control over personal data, across all its Azure SQL offerings.

15. **D** Azure Synapse Analytics

    Explanation: Azure Synapse Analytics is the service tailored for complex analytical workloads on large volumes of data. It combines big data and data warehousing, providing a unified analytics platform. With capabilities such as massive parallel processing (MPP) and on-demand query execution, it's well-suited to running extensive analytical queries and generating insights from historical datasets.

Scenario Exercises

Imagine you are working as a database administrator for a rapidly growing startup. The company is building a new web application that will handle a significant amount of user data, including usernames, passwords, and transaction data.

The team has decided to use Azure SQL Database for the application's database. The decision was based on the need for a scalable, fully managed database solution with minimal need for management overhead.

However, the team is new to Azure SQL Database. You have been tasked with creating a sample database and exploring some of the key features of Azure SQL Database.

Note: To complete this exercise, you will need an Azure subscription. If you don't have an Azure subscription, create a free account.

Exercise 1: Create a Database and Table

Step 1: Create an Azure SQL Database

1. Sign in to the Azure portal at portal.azure.com.

2. Click **Create a resource** at the top left of the screen (see Figure 2-26).

FIGURE 2-26 Creating a resource

3. Search for **SQL Database** and select it. See Figure 2-27.

FIGURE 2-27 Creating a SQL database

4. Click **Create** and fill in the details (shown in Figure 2-28) for your new database:

- **Subscription:** Choose your Azure subscription.
- **Resource group:** Create a new one or use an existing one.
- **Database name:** Choose a name for your database.
- **Server:** Create a new one or use an existing one.

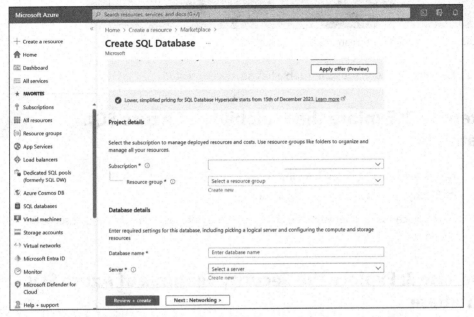

FIGURE 2-28 Creating the SQL database required details

5. After you've filled in the details, click **Review + Create** and then **Create**. Your Azure SQL Database is now being deployed.

Step 2: Create a Sample Table

1. Open SQL Server Management Studio (SSMS) or Azure Data Studio. For instructions on how to connect to Azure SQL Managed Instance using SSMS, see learn.microsoft.com/en-us/azure/azure-sql/database/connect-query-ssms?view=azuresql.

2. Connect to your database by entering your server's name and your login credentials.

3. Open a new query window and use the following SQL statement to create your Users table, as shown in Figure 2-29.

```scss
CREATE TABLE Users (
    UserID int,
    UserName nvarchar(50),
    Password nvarchar(50),
    TransactionData nvarchar(50)
);
```

FIGURE 2-29 SQL statement creating a Users table

4. Execute the query. Your Users table has now been created.

Exercise 2: Explore the Scalability of Azure SQL Database

1. Navigate to your SQL Database instance on the Azure portal.
2. Click Configure performance under Settings.
3. Here you can switch between the DTU and vCore purchasing models and observe the changes.

Exercise 3: Explore the Security Features of Azure SQL Database

1. In the Azure portal, navigate to your SQL Database instance.
2. Click Auditing under Security.
3. Toggle Auditing on, select your storage account, and set your retention (in days). Click Save.
4. Now, go back to Security and click Advance Threat Protection. Toggle the status to On and click Update.

Exercise 4: Explore Data Recovery in Azure SQL Database

1. In the Azure portal, navigate to your SQL Database instance.
2. Click Restore under Operations.
3. Choose a point in time to restore to and give your restored database a name. Click OK.

Remember to carefully read the documentation and understand the concepts and implications behind each action. This exercise is designed to provide hands-on experience and the understanding of key features of Azure SQL Database.

CHAPTER 3

Describe considerations for working with non-relational data on Azure

The contemporary era of cloud computing necessitates a profound understanding of various data types and storage options to effectively manage and utilize them. Non-relational data, also known as NoSQL, is a category of data that has seen substantial growth and acceptance in the last few years, particularly because of its flexibility, scalability, and performance advantages. This chapter will help you understand the nuances of working with non-relational data on Azure, Microsoft's comprehensive cloud platform.

In the first section, covering Skill 3.1, we'll explore the capabilities of Azure Storage, a durable, highly available, and massively scalable cloud storage solution. We'll delve into three distinct types of Azure Storage: Blob storage, File storage, and Table storage. Each of these has unique characteristics and use cases. For instance, Blob storage is suitable for unstructured data, File storage is for hierarchical file systems, and Table storage is for storing structured NoSQL data. You'll acquire the knowledge to determine the best Azure Storage option to meet your specific application needs.

Next, for Skill 3.2, we'll explore the capabilities of Azure Cosmos DB. With this globally distributed, multimodel database service, you can elastically and independently scale throughput and storage across any number of Azure's geographic regions. We'll inspect the potential use cases for Cosmos DB, shedding light on why and when you might opt for this database service. Additionally, we'll discuss the various APIs that Cosmos DB offers for interacting with data. Understanding these APIs will help you leverage the full power of Cosmos DB and integrate it seamlessly with a range of applications and services.

The exploration of Azure's non-relational data capabilities is not just about data storage; it's about understanding how to best use these technologies to build robust, scalable, and cost-effective applications. While these topics may seem complex, with focused study and practice, you will be well-equipped to navigate Azure's non-relational data storage landscape. Let's begin this journey of discovery together!

Skills covered in this chapter:

- Skill 3.1 Describe capabilities of Azure Storage
- Skill 3.2 Describe capabilities and features of Azure Cosmos DB

Skill 3.1: Describe capabilities of Azure Storage

This section will deepen your understanding of Azure Storage, one of the core services provided by Microsoft's cloud platform, Azure. It's crucial to comprehend the Azure Storage capabilities because Azure Storage forms the foundation of data management in Azure. Azure Storage is not only durable, secure, and scalable but also offers various types of storage, each designed to address specific business needs.

The types of Azure Storage we will focus on in this section are Blob storage, File storage, and Table storage. Blob storage is designed to handle a large amount of unstructured data, such as text or binary data. File storage offers shared storage for applications using the standard SMB protocol, and Table storage is Azure's NoSQL offering for the schema-less storage of structured data.

Understanding the capabilities of each of these storage types, their potential use cases, and their limitations is an essential part of designing efficient and effective data solutions in Azure. By the end of this section, you'll have a solid understanding of these services, empowering you to choose and implement the best Azure Storage service for your specific application requirements.

Remember, while the breadth of Azure Storage may seem overwhelming at first, a methodical approach to learning and understanding each component's functionality can simplify the process significantly. Stay focused, remain curious, and let's dive into the fascinating world of Azure Storage.

> **This skill covers how to:**
> - Describe Azure Blob storage
> - Describe Azure Data Lake Storage Gen2
> - Describe Azure File storage
> - Describe Azure Table storage

Describe Azure Blob storage

Azure Blob storage is a service for storing a large amount of unstructured object data, such as text or binary data. Blob storage can handle all sorts of data such as documents, media files, application installers, and data for backup, restore, archive, and disaster recovery purposes.

Blob storage can manage blobs that are hundreds of gigabytes in size. This scalability, along with its cost-effectiveness and durability, makes it an excellent choice for data that must be readily available for access from anywhere in the world.

Figure 3-1 represents the Blob storage hierarchy.

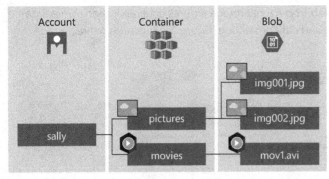

FIGURE 3-1 Blob storage hierarchy

Blob storage architecture

Azure Blob storage is organized into storage accounts and containers, akin to a file system's organization into drives and folders. Each storage account can contain an unlimited number of containers, and each container can store an unlimited number of blobs.

STORAGE ACCOUNT

The storage account provides a unique namespace in Azure for all the data you will be storing. Every object that you store in Azure Storage has an address, and this address includes the name of your storage account.

Here are the key features of the storage account:

- **Variety of storage options:** Azure Storage supports different types of data objects such as blobs, files, queues, tables, and disks, as shown in Figure 3-2.

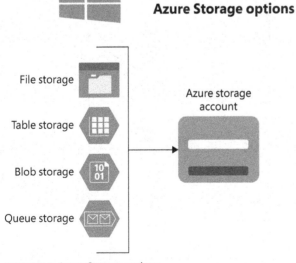

FIGURE 3-2 Azure Storage options

- **High durability and availability:** Azure Storage ensures data replication across data-centers for high availability and data protection. Figure 3-3 illustrates Azure Storage data replication.

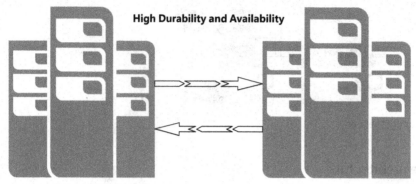

FIGURE 3-3 Datacenter replication

- **Security and compliance:** Features such as Azure Active Directory authentication and role-based access control bolster security. Figure 3-4 shows a flowchart of the security features in an Azure Storage account.

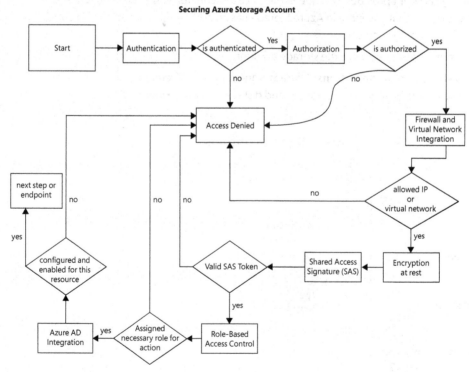

FIGURE 3-4 Security features in an Azure Storage account

- **Scalability:** Azure Storage is capable of handling large volumes of data with its scalability options, as shown in Figure 3-5.

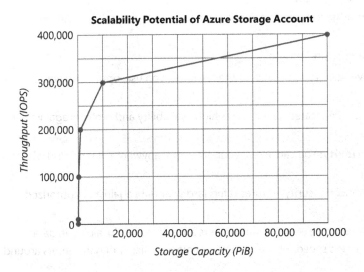

Scalability Potential of Azure Storage Account

FIGURE 3-5 Scalability potential of an Azure Storage account

- This graph reveals the remarkable scalability potential of Azure Storage accounts, demonstrating their ability to handle massive amounts of data and high-traffic scenarios.

Here are the highlights of scalability in Azure Storage accounts:

- **Massive storage potential:** Azure Storage accounts can scale to more than 80 PB, accommodating vast datasets and supporting significant growth.
- **High performance:** With peak throughput exceeding 20,000 IOPS, these accounts can efficiently handle heavy workloads and numerous concurrent requests.
- **Independent scalability:** Storage capacity and throughput can be scaled independently, allowing you to tailor the account to specific needs.
- **Flexible options:** You can choose between standard and premium storage accounts, balancing cost with performance requirements.

Here are the scalability features available for Azure Storage accounts:

- **Tier up:** You can upgrade to premium storage for increased performance and capacity.
- **Add storage:** You can increase capacity without impacting performance by adding more petabytes to your existing account.

Here are the applications that can use Azure Storage:

- **Web applications:** You can store static and dynamic content with high availability and scalability.

- **Media streaming:** You can deliver high-quality video and music streams worldwide with efficient data access.
- **Big data analytics:** You can process massive datasets effectively with reliable storage and high throughput.
- **Machine learning:** You can train and store machine learning models with robust infrastructure.

Here are the benefits of Azure Storage:

- **Cost-effectiveness:** You pay only for the resources you use, optimizing your storage expenses.
- **Data resilience:** Replicated data ensures high availability and protects against data loss.
- **Global accessibility:** You can access your data from anywhere in the world with low latency.
- **Security:** Advanced security features safeguard your data against unauthorized access.
- **Global reach:** Data can be stored in datacenters around the world, aiding in data localization and access speed. Figure 3-6 shows a map of Microsoft datacenters around the world.

FIGURE 3-6 Microsoft datacenters around the world

- **Cost-effectiveness:** Various pricing tiers are available to suit different requirements and budgets. Table 3-1 compares the pricing tiers for Azure Storage accounts.

TABLE 3-1 Azure Storage account pricing tiers

Feature	Hot	Cool	Archive
Storage	Hotly accessed data	Infrequently accessed data	Rarely accessed data
Minimum storage duration	None	30 days	180 days
Storage cost per GB/month	$0.022 to $0.028	$0.010 to $0.014	$0.002 to $0.003
Retrieval cost per GB	$0.004 to $0.006	$0.010 to $0.014	$0.12 to $0.16
Write cost per GB	$0.005 to $0.007	$0.010 to $0.014	$0.012 to $0.016
API request cost	$0.0004	$0.0004	$0.0004
Recommended use cases	Frequently accessed data, applications, websites	Backups, disaster recovery, archives	Long-term archival data, rarely accessed data
Data access latency	Low	Lower than Hot	Lowest

CONTAINER

Containers in Azure Blob storage are similar to directories in a file system. They provide a way to organize sets of blobs, such as text files, images, or other media. A blob is a file of any type and size, and there are three types: block blobs, append blobs, and page blobs. Containers are ideal for grouping blobs in a systematic way, making data management more efficient and accessible.

Here are the key characteristics of containers:

- **Access control:** Containers can have different access levels such as private, blob-level public access, or container-level public access.
- **Scalability:** They can store a massive number of blobs, including large blobs, making them highly scalable.
- **Security:** Containers can be integrated with Azure Active Directory and other Azure security features.
- Figure 3-7 shows an Azure Storage account with multiple containers.

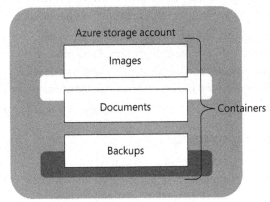

FIGURE 3-7 Multiple containers, each containing a different type of blob

Types of blobs

The versatility of Azure Blob storage is primarily due to its ability to support different types of blobs. Each blob type is optimized for a specific kind of operation or use case, making blob storage highly adaptable and applicable to various scenarios. Let's delve into each blob type more extensively.

- **Block blobs:** Block blobs are designed to handle a large amount of data efficiently. A single block blob can contain up to 50,000 blocks of up to 100 MB each, which means a single block blob can handle data up to approximately 4.75 TB. Block blobs are ideal for scenarios where data size can range from small to massive, such as serving images to documents directly to a browser or storing backup files, media files for streaming, and high-resolution images.

  Moreover, Azure supports uploading large block blobs in parallel, so you get efficient data transfer. Block blobs also support various operations such as adding, uploading, committing, and deleting blocks.

- **Append blobs:** Append blobs, as the name suggests, are optimized for append operations, making them the perfect choice for logging data from virtual machines or storing telemetry data. They are similar to block blobs but are designed to handle append operations efficiently. An append blob can be modified by appending blocks, but blocks cannot be updated or deleted, providing a simple and efficient solution for scenarios where data needs to be only added.

  These blobs can handle data up to approximately 195 GB and are highly useful for operations such as capturing the output of log files.

- **Page blobs:** Page blobs are designed for random access scenarios and can support up to 8 TB of data. They provide the ability to read/write pages and are ideal for scenarios where random read/write operations are frequent. A primary example of page blob usage is Azure's implementation of virtual hard drives (VHDs) for its virtual machines. In the case of Azure VMs, the VM operating system drives and any additional data drives are all stored as page blobs.

  Page blobs allow transactional changes, meaning you can modify, add, and update a range of pages within a blob independently, a feature that makes them perfect for serving as disks for Azure VMs or other services that require heavy read/write operations.

Understanding these different blob types and their ideal use cases will help you make informed decisions when implementing solutions using Azure Blob storage. Remember that the choice of blob type will significantly impact the performance, scalability, and cost of your Azure-based applications, so take the time to understand these details so you can utilize Azure blob storage most effectively.

Understanding access tiers in Azure Blob storage

Access tiers in Azure Blob storage are policies that you can set at the account level or at the individual blob level. They help optimize costs by storing your database based on how often you access it. There are three access tiers in Azure Blob storage: Hot, Cool, and Archive.

- **Hot access tier:** The Hot access tier is optimized for storing data that is accessed frequently. This tier has higher storage costs compared to the Cool and Archive tiers, but the costs for accessing data (read/write operations) and transactional costs are lower. Therefore, it's best to use this tier for data that needs to be really accessible and frequently read and listed.

- **Cool access tier:** The Cool tier, on the other hand, is optimized for storing data that is infrequently accessed and stored for at least 30 days. The storage costs for the Cool tier are lower than the Hot tier, but the cost for accessing data and transaction costs is higher. This tier is perfect for short-term backup and disaster recovery datasets.

- **Archive access tier:** The Archive access tier has the lowest storage cost but the highest data retrieval costs. Data in the Archive tier is offline and not readily accessible. Therefore, this tier is best for data that can tolerate several hours of retrieval latency and is accessed less than once a year. This tier is suitable for long-term backup, secondary backup, and archival datasets.

It's possible to change the access tier of a blob at any time. The change happens immediately when changing to the Hot or Cool tier. However, when changing to the Archive tier, it might take several hours for Azure to move the data to the offline Archive storage. Similarly, when rehydrating data from the Archive tier to the Hot or Cool tier, there is a delay as Azure must retrieve the data from offline storage.

Please note that transitioning between tiers incurs a cost, so it's essential to consider the trade-offs between access latency, cost, and how often you access your data when choosing the appropriate tier.

By understanding these access tiers and their optimal use cases, you'll be better equipped to manage your data storage in a cost-effective manner, aligning your Azure blob storage with your specific requirements. Always remember, the optimal tier depends on your data access patterns and overall business needs.

> **NEED MORE REVIEW?** **AZURE BLOB STORAGE**
>
> You can learn more about Azure Blob storage at *learn.microsoft.com/en-us/training/modules/explore-provision-deploy-non-relational-data-services-azure/2-azure-blob-storage.*

Describe Azure Data Lake Storage Gen2

Azure Data Lake Storage Gen2 is more than just another data storage option; it's a large-scale data lake solution tailored for big data analytics. Gen2 enhances the core capabilities of Azure Data Lake Storage Gen1, coupling the benefits of Azure blob storage capabilities with additional and robust data analytics features. As you venture into this, you'll uncover the depth and breadth of features designed to assist you.

Key enhancements of Azure Data Lake (Gen2)

Azure Data Lake Storage, in its second-generation incarnation, has significantly improved features. Designed to be the optimum solution for big data analytics, Gen2 not only augments its original functionalities but also integrates seamlessly with various Azure services. Here are the key enhancements that distinguish Azure Data Lake Storage Gen2 from its predecessor:

- **Performance:** The second version has enhanced data analytics performance and management ease due to Azure Blob storage capabilities.

- **Hierarchical namespaces:** This unique feature facilitates data organization and fine-tuned data access management. With this, you can efficiently manage and organize your data into folders and subfolders.

- **Security:** Enhanced security features include POSIX-compliant access control lists (ACLs) and Azure Active Directory (Azure AD)–based authentication and role-based access control. (POSIX is a set of standards defined by the IEEE to ensure compatibility between operating systems. The intent is that developers can write applications that are portable, meaning they can be run on various operating systems without modifications. An ACL is a list of permissions attached to an object, such as a file or directory. These permissions dictate what actions a user, or a group of users, can perform on that object.)

- **Scalability and durability:** Built on Azure Blob storage, Azure Data Lake Storage Gen2 guarantees high availability, disaster recovery, and backup.

Architecture of Azure Data Lake Storage Gen2

Azure Data Lake Storage Gen2 (often referred to as ADL Gen2) is a comprehensive and intricate platform that has been intricately designed to handle vast datasets, especially when big data analytics is in play. To truly harness its capabilities, understanding its architecture is fundamental. So, let's guide you through the architectural framework of ADLS Gen2:

- **Foundational principles:** Azure Data Lake Storage Gen2 extends the capabilities of Azure Blob storage. Essentially, it combines the scalable and cost-efficient nature of Blob storage with big data analytics capabilities, resulting in a powerful hybrid.

- **Hierarchical namespace:** At the heart of ADLS Gen2's architecture is the hierarchical namespace. You can organize objects (such as files and directories) into a hierarchy, similar to a file system. Operations such as renaming or deleting directories become atomic, which optimizes big data workloads.

  - **Storage account:** This is the apex of the organizational structure in ADLS Gen2. Every storage account possesses a unique namespace that is used to address both Blob and data lake storage data in that account.

  - **Containers:** Within storage accounts are containers, functioning almost like directories in traditional file systems. They group sets of blobs and can be used to organize data based on projects, departments, or data types.

  - **Blob:** Every data piece in Azure Data Lake Storage Gen2 is essentially a blob. You'll deal with large files broken into chunks, with each chunk being a blob. These blobs can be further categorized into block blobs and append blobs.

  - **Azure Active Directory (Azure AD):** With Azure AD, you get seamless integration, allowing you to set up authentication and authorization mechanisms for your data.

- **Role-based access control (RBAC):** Assign roles and manage access at granular levels, ensuring that the right people have the right permissions.
- **POSIX-compliant ACLs:** Further refine data access with POSIX-compliant ACLs. This is a game-changer for big data processing needs, offering precision access control.

- **Data integration:** Azure Data Lake Storage Gen2 smoothly integrates with various Azure processing solutions, such as Azure Databricks, Azure HDInsight, and Azure Data Factory. This integration means that once your data is stored, processing and analyzing it become more streamlined.

- **Performance:** Being built upon the foundational principles of Azure Blob storage, ADLS Gen2 offers massive scalability, high availability, and robust data analytics performance. Features like multiprotocol access on the same account ensure that you can use the Blob object store and the data lake store in a congruent manner, optimizing your data analytics tasks.

Figure 3-8 shows the architecture of Azure Data Lake Storage Gen2.

```
Storage Account (Top-tier)
|
|----Container (Organizational segments)
|    |
|    |----Blob (Chunks of data)
|    |----Blob
|    L___...
|
|----Container
L___...
```

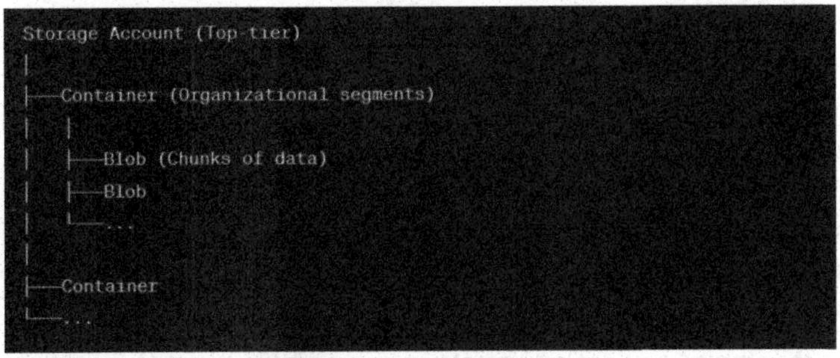

FIGURE 3-8 Azure Data Lake Storage Gen2 architecture

The architecture of Azure Data Lake Storage Gen2 is a testament to Azure's commitment to offering a structured yet flexible environment for big data analytics. As you immerse yourself deeper into the intricacies of ADLS Gen2, you'll discover that its architectural choices serve both your present and future data needs.

> **NEED MORE REVIEW? AZURE DATA LAKE STORAGE GEN2**
>
> You can learn more about Azure Data Lake Storage Gen2 at *learn.microsoft.com/en-us/ training/modules/explore-provision-deploy-non-relational-data-services-azure/3-azure-data-lake-gen2.*

Describe Azure File storage

Azure File storage, a service provided by Microsoft Azure, offers managed file shares in the cloud that are accessible via the industry-standard Server Message Block (SMB) protocol or Network Files System (NFS) protocol. This means you can mount Azure file shares from anywhere, whether inside your cloud-based virtual machine (VM) or directly from your on-premises workstations.

Key Features of Azure File storage

Azure File storage allows multiple applications or users to share the same files, making it an ideal choice for many applications, development and testing environments, analytics, reporting, and more.

Key features include the following:

- There is integration with Azure Backup and Azure File Sync for cloud tiering of on-premise file shares.
- Share snapshots provide a way to make incremental backups of on-premise file shares.
- Azure File shares can be used with Windows, Linux, and macOS.

Architecture of Azure File storage

Azure File storage is designed to provide scalable and secure file shares in the cloud. The service is built on a foundation of storage accounts, shares, directories, and files, which together create a hierarchical organization system.

- **Storage account:** At the root of the Azure File storage architecture is the storage account. A storage account provides a unique namespace by your Azure Storage data that's accessible from anywhere in the world over HTTP or HTTPS. Each storage account holds the settings for that account, such as the Azure region, the replication policy, and the access tier (premium or standard).
- **File shares:** Within the storage account, you create one or more file shares. A file share represents an SMB file share in Azure. Each file share can be up to 5 TB in size, but you can have multiple file shares within a storage account.
- **Directories:** Within a file share, you can create directories. Directories in Azure Storage behave similarly to directories in a traditional file system, helping you organize and manage your files effectively. It's important to note that directories in Azure File storage are not the same as Blob storage folders, even though they serve a similar organizational purpose.
- **Files:** Finally, within directories, you store your files. Individual files in Azure File storage can be up to 1 TB in size. Just like a file on your local file system, a file in Azure File storage has properties (such as its size and last-modified time), metadata (name-value pairs), and content.
- **Accessing Azure File storage:** You can access Azure File storage using the SMB or REST protocol. The REST interface allows access from anywhere over HTTP or HTTPS, while the SMB protocol allows you to mount the file share on Windows, Linux, or macOS machines.

Figure 3-9 illustrates the Azure File storage architecture.

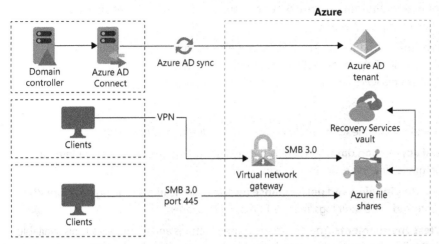

FIGURE 3-9 Azure File storage architecture

By understanding the architecture of Azure File storage, you'll be better prepared to design and implement an effective storage strategy that maximizes scalability, performance, and security.

Azure File Sync

One of the most compelling features of Azure File storage is its integration with Azure File Sync. Azure File Sync allows for the centralization of files shares in Azure while maintaining the compatibility and accessibility of an on-premises file server.

Azure File Sync uses a sync group, which defines the sync topology for a set of files. The sync group contains a cloud endpoint (an Azure File share) and one or more server endpoints (a path on your Windows Server). Changes to the file share are then tracked and propagated to connected servers via Azure File Sync, and vice versa.

This process offers several benefits:

- **Multisite access:** It gives you cloud-based access to your data while maintaining local access to the same dataset across your Windows Servers.
- **Cloud tiering:** Infrequently used or accessed files can be tiered to Azure Files, freeing up on-premise storage.
- **Integrated cloud backup:** Azure File shares can be protected using Azure Backup.

SECURITY AND ACCESS CONTROL

Azure File storage provides multiple levels of security:

- **Firewalls and virtual networks:** You can restrict access to your Azure File storage at the network layer.
- **Access keys:** You can grant access to your Azure File storage using shared keys.
- **Shared access signatures (SAS):** You can provide secure, delegated access to resources in your storage account through SAS tokens.

- **Azure Active Directory (Azure AD):** You can use Azure AD credentials in a domain environment for SBM access.
- **Encryption:** Data stored in Azure File storage is encrypted at rest using Microsoft Storage Service Encryption (SSE), and data transmitted to/from Azure File storage is secured using SSL/TLS.

USE CASES

Azure File storage is suitable for a variety of use cases, including the following:

- **Shared application data:** You can use Azure File storage to replace or supplement on-premises file servers or NAS devices.
- **Diagnostics logging and performance metrics:** Applications running on Azure VMs can write and store their logs/metrics to Azure File shares.
- **Dev/test environments:** You can create shared settings and diagnostics tools available to all VMs in a development or test environment.

With an understanding of these Azure File storage details, you will be able to leverage Azure File storage's capabilities effectively. By incorporating Azure File storage in your cloud architecture, you can maintain a flexible and scalable data sharing and storage strategy.

> **NEED MORE REVIEW?** **AZURE FILE STORAGE**
>
> You can learn more about Azure File storage at *learn.microsoft.com/en-us/training/modules/ explore-provision-deploy-non-relational-data-services-azure/4-azure-files.*

Describe Azure Table storage

Navigating the world of structured, non-relational data can seem daunting. Enter Azure Table storage, part of Azure's rich storage ecosystem. This NoSQL datastore embraces the schema-less design philosophy, ensuring that as your data needs evolve, your storage can too. Let's walk through this together so you can see what Azure Table storage offers you.

Understanding Azure Table storage

Azure Table storage is your go-to NoSQL data service for handling vast amounts of structured data. Instead of locking you into a rigid structure, it offers the flexibility to evolve your data schema as your application grows. Imagine being in a scenario where you need to add columns to your data on the fly. That's where Azure Table shines for you.

Your Building Blocks

Azure Table storage operates around three fundamental elements, tailor-made for your flexible data needs:

- **Tables:** Think of these as your main storage spaces. Each table is a unique collection of entities, helping you segment and organize your data effortlessly.

- **Entities:** These are your data rows, but with a twist. Every entity in Azure Table storage can possess its unique set of properties, allowing you to customize data points as you go.
- **Properties:** These are your actual data points, structured as key-value pairs. You can equip each entity with up to 252 properties.

Figure 3-10 illustrates the building blocks of Azure Table storage.

```
Table (Your primary storage space)
|
└──Entity (Your individual data points)
   |
   ├──Property (E.g., Name: "Age", Value: "30")
   ├──Property (E.g., Name: "City", Value: "London")
   └── ... (Tailor them as you wish)
```

FIGURE 3-10 Azure Table storage building blocks

With Azure Table storage, you're not just accessing a NoSQL data store. You're stepping into an adaptable platform crafted especially for dynamic scenarios. If you're looking to strike that sweet spot between flexibility and scalability, Azure Table storage is your answer. Dive into the schema-less realm, and let Azure Table storage be your trusted companion.

> **NEED MORE REVIEW?** **AZURE TABLE STORAGE**
>
> You can learn more about Azure Table storage at *learn.microsoft.com/en-us/training/modules/ explore-provision-deploy-non-relational-data-services-azure/5-azure-tables*.

Skill 3.2: Describe capabilities and features of Azure Cosmos DB

In the ever-evolving cloud ecosystem, data is as diverse as it is vast. While traditional relational databases have their strengths, the modern digital landscape often demands more. Enter Azure Cosmos DB, a globally distributed, multimodel database service that's crafted to cater to contemporary applications. As we venture through this section, you'll unravel the myriad capabilities of Azure Cosmos DB, its use cases, and the intricate features it offers to developers and businesses alike.

Azure Cosmos DB isn't just a database; it's a solution sculpted for the global stage. It promises elastic scalability, unwavering performance, and a plethora of APIs to interact with multiple data models. As we delve deeper, you'll grasp how Azure Cosmos DB not only tackles the challenges of today's data demands but also elegantly prepares you for the future.

From understanding the primary use cases that drive organizations to adopt this versatile platform to exploring the various APIs it supports, Skill 3.2 is your guidepost. In this section, you'll appreciate how Azure Cosmos DB bridges the gaps of traditional databases and offers a seamless, globally distributed solution that resonates with today's digital-first ethos.

This skill covers how to:

- Identify use cases for Azure Cosmos DB
- Describe Azure Cosmos DB APIs

Identify use cases for Azure Cosmos DB

Azure Cosmos DB, Microsoft's globally distributed, multimodel database service, boasts a myriad of features designed for today's fast-paced digital world. It's not just about strong data; it's about doing so with unmatched flexibility, reliability, and scalability. But where exactly does Azure Cosmos DB shine? Let's dive into the prominent use cases and, through examples, understand how this service fits into real-world scenarios.

- **Global distribution:** Azure Cosmos DB is designed with a global audience in mind. If you're aiming to provide low latency and a seamless user experience across the globe, this is your solution. Think of your vision for an international e-commerce platform. With Cosmos DB, your customers in Europe, Asia, or America can have equally fast access, ensuring prompt product searches and swift checkouts.

- **Scalable and flexible application:** Anticipate varied workloads? Cosmos DB is your ally, letting you scale on-demand without the hiccups of downtime. Consider your dream of launching an app that might go viral overnight. Even with a sudden influx of users, Azure Cosmos DB seamlessly ensures your new users get the same great experience as the first user did.

- **Real-time IoT and telemetry:** If you're venturing into the realm of IoT, with devices emitting streams of real-time data, Cosmos stands ready. Picture your smart home solution where every device, from thermostats to security cameras, sends data. Azure Cosmos DB can process this in real time, allowing you to offer instant feedback or actions to your users.

- **Personalization and AI:** Personalization is the future, and with Cosmos DB, you can store and process vast user data for AI-driven recommendations. Envision your music streaming services. Each song a user plays informs the next suggestion, making their playlist truly personal. Cosmos DB's fast data retrieval ensures those recommendations appear in a heartbeat.

- **Multimodel and multi-API:** Should your projects require multiple data models, Cosmos DB offers you the flexibility of multiple APIs for diverse data interactions. Your health portal could leverage graph data for patient relations, document data for medical histories, and add key-value pairs for user settings, all harmoniously under the Cosmos DB umbrella.

- **High availability:** For those mission-critical applications where downtime isn't an option, Cosmos DB offers robustness with its high availability. Envision a hospital management system that requires 24/7 uptime. With Cosmos DB's multiregion replication, even if one region faces issues, the system remains operational, safeguarding crucial medical processes.

- **Data migration:** One of the subtle advantages of Azure Cosmos DB lies in its accommodating nature when it comes to migration. If you've been pondering migrating from an existing database or another NoSQL solution, you're in for a smoother journey. Let's say you've been running a legacy e-commerce site on MongoDB. With Azure Cosmos DB's compatibility with the MongoDB API, you can migrate without having to redesign your entire application. This allows you to utilize the global distribution and scalability features of Cosmos DB without a cumbersome migration process.

- **Security and compliance:** In a world where data breaches make headlines, you might be striving for tighter security protocols. Azure Cosmos DB comes equipped with advanced security features and compliance certifications, ensuring your data remains in safe hands. If you're building a financial application, the built-in encryption, both at rest and in transit, combined with role-based access control, offers you the peace of mind that sensitive financial data is protected against potential threats.

- **Build responsive and real-time web applications:** The digital age has ushered in an era of instant gratification. If your projects involve real-time web apps, Cosmos DB's low-latency data access ensures that your application remains snappy and responsive. Imagine developing a live sports score website. As the match progresses and scores update in real time, your website can reflect these changes instantaneously, ensuring fans are always up-to-date, thanks to Cosmos DB's swift read and write capabilities.

- **Multitenancy and data isolation:** If your aspirations include building multitenant applications where each tenant's data needs to be isolated from others, Azure Cosmos DB offers robust support for such architectures, ensuring data privacy and operational efficiency. Visualize a SaaS-based CRM tool you're designing. Each business that uses your tool gets its isolated data environment, ensuring their data doesn't mix with others while still maintaining optimal performance.

Azure Cosmos DB is not just a database; it's an expansive toolkit waiting for you to harness. The myriad use cases available offer not only solutions to contemporary challenges but also open avenues for innovative application. Whether you're a beginner or a seasoned developer, it's your guide, your reference, and your mentor, ensuring you unlock the full spectrum of Azure Cosmos DB capabilities.

> **NEED MORE REVIEW? AZURE COSMOS DB**
>
> You can learn more about Azure Cosmos DB at *learn.microsoft.com/en-us/training/modules/ explore-non-relational-data-stores-azure/2-describe-azure-cosmos-db*.

Describe Azure Cosmos DB APIs

While navigating the digital realm, developers often grapple with the challenge of accommodating diverse data structures. What if there were a tool that could converse fluently with varying data types, all while maintaining the robustness and scalability that modern applications demand? Enter Azure Cosmos DB and its wide array of APIs.

Azure Cosmos isn't just your average database service. Its unique selling point is its multimodel capability, allowing you to interact with data in several formats, from document to columnar to graph. At the heart of this versatility are the APIs that Azure Cosmos DB supports. These APIs empower you to harness different data models seamlessly and tailor the database to your application's needs rather than forcing your application to fit a specific database mold.

In the sections to come, you'll embark on a journey through these APIs, understanding their intricacies, benefits, and real-world applications. Whether you're molding JSON documents, migrating from MongoDB, or diving into the interconnected world of graph databases, there's an API tailored just for you.

Get ready to dive into this powerful facet of Azure Cosmos DB, unraveling its potential to revolutionize the way you perceive and interact with databases.

Core (SQL) API

At its heart, Azure Cosmos DB started with its native API, designed primarily for semi-structured JSON documents. This API fuses the NoSQL world with familiar SQL querying capabilities, granting developers the flexibility of JSON with the familiarity of SQL operations.

These are its advantages:

- **Flexibility:** Easily manage and query JSON documents.
- **Familiar syntax:** Utilize SQL-like queries to manage your data.

Suppose you have a collection of articles stored as JSON documents, as shown in Figure 3-11.

```
{
  "id": "123",
  "title": "Introduction to Azure",
  "author": "Jane Doe",
  "date_published": "2023-07-21"
}
```

FIGURE 3-11 Article stored as a JSON document

Figure 3-12 shows the SQL-like query you use to retrieve all the articles by Jane Doe.

```
SELECT * FROM Articles a WHERE a.author = 'Jane Doe'
```

FIGURE 3-12 SQL-like query to retrieve articles

MongoDB API

Migrating from MongoDB with the Cosmos DB's MongoDB API ensures that the transition is seamless. This compatibility allows applications already using MongoDB to migrate without substantial changes.

Here are the advantages of using the API:

- **Smooth migration:** Existing MongoDB applications can be moved with minimal modifications.
- **Global scale:** Harness Cosmos DB's distribution and scalability features for your MongoDB data.

If you have a MongoDB collection for user profiles, as shown in Figure 3-13, you can use the MongoDB shell with a typical query, as shown in Figure 3-14, to fetch the user detail.

```
{
    "username": "johnD",
    "email": "john.doe@email.com",
    "join_date": "2021-01-15"
}
```

FIGURE 3-13 JSON representation of a user profile

```
db.users.find({"username": "johnD"})
```

FIGURE 3-14 Typical query done in the MongoDB shell

Cassandra API

For applications already entrenched in Apache Cassandra's column-family data model, Cosmos DB provides the Cassandra API, ensuring that migration and integration are straightforward.

Here are the advantages of using the Cassandra API:

- **Native support:** Directly interact with column-family data models without needing to reshape your data.
- **Enhanced performance:** Leverage Azure's robust infrastructure for better responsiveness and uptime.

Assuming you have a table for tracking user activity, as shown in Figure 3-15, to fetch the activity for a specific user, you'd use the select statement shown in Figure 3-16.

```
CREATE TABLE user_activity (
    username TEXT,
    activity_date DATE,
    activity TEXT,
    PRIMARY KEY (username, activity_date)
);
```

FIGURE 3-15 Table for tracking user activity

```
SELECT * FROM user_activity WHERE username = 'johnD';
```

FIGURE 3-16 Fetching the activity for a specific user

Azure Table API

Aimed at applications leveraging Azure Table storage, the Azure Table API ensures that transitioning to Cosmos DB is smooth, offering a more potent suite of features and capabilities.

Here are the advantages of the Azure Table API:

- **Seamless transition:** Migrate from Azure Table storage with ease.
- **Advanced features:** Access Cosmos DB's advanced toolset, from global distribution to automatic scaling.

Gremlin (Graphic) API

When it comes to modeling intricate, interconnected data, the Gremlin API stands out. Ideal for applications delving into graph databases, this API provides tools to manage and traverse relationships with efficiency.

- **Complex relationships:** The Gremlin API is perfectly suited for applications such as social networks, recommendation systems, or any other platform requiring intricate data connections.
- **Powerful query:** The Gremlin query language allows for in-depth traversals, ensuring detailed insight for your graph data.

Each of these APIs illustrates Azure Cosmos DB's commitment to providing developers with versatile tools tailored to their specific needs. As you venture deeper into your projects, remember: Azure Cosmos DB's API suite ensures that you have the right tool for the job regardless of your data model or system.

EXAM TIP

When answering questions related to Azure Storage and Cosmos DB on the exam, always consider the data type (structured versus unstructured), data access patterns (frequency, latency requirements), and scalability needs. Understanding the unique characteristics and benefits of each Azure Storage type and the Cosmos DB API can help you select the right solution for a given scenario.

Here are some examples:

- For large volumes of unstructured data such as images or videos, Azure Blob storage is commonly the go-to solution.
- When you encounter questions about globally distributed applications requiring low-latency and multiregion replication, Cosmos DB should be top of mind.
- If there's mention of structured, non-relational data in a key-value format, think of Azure Table storage.

- For hierarchical data structures ideal for big data analytics, remember Azure Data Lake Storage Gen2.

By grounding your knowledge in real-world applications and distinct use cases, you'll be better positioned to answer exam questions accurately and confidently.

Remember to revisit this tip before your exam. It will serve as a guiding principle to quickly and effectively reason through storage-related questions!

Chapter summary

This summary provides an overview of the main points and details covered in this chapter, facilitating quick revision and recall.

- Explored Azure Storage
  - Provides scalable, durable, and highly available storage solutions
  - Addresses specific requirements through various data storage types
- Explored Blob storage
  - Optimized for storing massive amount of unstructured data
  - Different access tiers (Hot, Cool, Archive) based on access frequency and retention periods
- Explored File storage
  - Allows shred storage using the standard SMB protocol
  - Supports both on-premises and Azure-based SMB clients
- Explored Table storage
  - Designed for structured, non-relational data in a key-value format
  - Ideal for storing large amounts of non-relational data that doesn't require complex joins or relations
- Explored Azure Data Lake Storage Gen2
  - Hierarchical file system optimized for big data analytics
  - Integration capabilities with Azure Databricks, Azure HDInsight, and Azure Synapse Analytics
- Looked at Azure Cosmos DB use cases
  - Globally distributed, multimodel database service
  - Suitable for mission-critical applications, including IoT, AI, and mobile apps
  - Ensures data is available in close proximity to users worldwide
- Explored Azure Cosmos DB APIs
  - **Core (SQL) API:** Default, JSON-based
  - **MongoDB API:** Supports MongoDB workloads
  - **Gremlin (Graph) API:** For graph databases

- **Cassandra API:** Compatible with Cassandra workloads
- **Table API:** For applications requiring wide-column stores

Auto-scaling, partitioning, and global distribution features optimize performance and scalability.

Thought experiment

Your company is developing a new web portal where users can upload and share videos. You're tasked with choosing the right Azure service for storing these videos.

1. Which Azure Storage solution would be the most cost-effective and suitable for storing large amounts of video data?

    A. Azure Table storage

    B. Azure Cosmos DB

    C. Azure File storage

    D. Azure Blob storage

    The IT department of your organization is looking to replace their traditional shared drivers with a cloud-based solution that integrates easily with the existing on-premises Active Directory setup.

2. Which Azure service should they consider?

    A. Azure Blob storage

    B. Azure Cosmos DB

    C. Azure Data Lake Storage Gen2

    D. Azure File storage

    A mobile application development company needs a globally distributed database solution that can automatically replicate data across multiple regions and provide low-latency data access.

3. Which Azure database service fits this requirement?

    A. Azure SQL Database

    B. Azure Cosmos DB

    C. Azure Blob storage

    D. Azure Table storage

    A startup specializing in graph-based analytics and visualization wants to store a vast number of interconnected datasets. They're looking for a compatible API within Azure services.

4. Which Azure Cosmos DB API would best cater to their needs?

    A. Core (SQL) API

    B. MongoDB API

C. Gremlin (Graph) API

D. Cassandra API

An organization has accumulated years of logs and raw telemetry data, which they rarely access but need to retain for compliance. They are seeking an Azure Storage tier that's both cost-effective and suitable for this purpose.

5. What tier of Azure Blob storage should they opt for?

A. Hot

B. Cool

C. Premium

D. Archive

A financial firm is exploring Azure Storage options to store transaction records. The records need to be organized in a key-value format and don't require any complex relational operations.

6. Which Azure Storage option is most appropriate for this requirement?

A. Azure File storage

B. Azure Table storage

C. Azure Cosmos DB with Core (SQL) API

D. Azure Blob storage

A media agency is in the process of creating a backup solution for its large image and video files. The company wants a solution where these files can be directly mounted to virtual machines when required.

7. Which Azure Storage solution should the media agency consider?

A. Azure Data Lake Storage Gen2

B. Azure Blob storage

C. Azure Table storage

D. Azure File storage

A gaming company is building a new online multiplayer game. The company needs a database solution that can handle rapid writes and reads of small amounts of data with extremely low latency.

8. Which Azure service would be optimal for such requirements?

A. Azure SQL Database

B. Azure Cosmos DB

C. Azure Blob storage

D. Azure Table storage

A research organization needs to store a vast amount of data for big data analytics. The data must be organized hierarchically, and the solution should also support analytics and AI workloads.

9. Which Azure Storage option is the most fitting for these needs?

A. Azure Blob storage

B. Azure Cosmos DB

C. Azure Data Lake Storage Gen2

D. Azure File storage

An e-commerce platform is looking for a flexible database service that can grow dynamically without the need to pre-allocate database throughput. The service adapts as the request volume changes.

10. Which Azure database service should the company utilize?

A. Azure SQL Database

B. Azure Cosmos DB with auto-scale throughput

C. Azure Blob storage

D. Azure Table storage

Your organization wants to migrate its application logs to Azure for analysis. You are expecting large volumes of logs daily but plan to query only the most recent ones frequently.

11. Which storage tier in Azure Blob storage best suits this requirement?

A. Hot

B. Cool

C. Premium

D. Archive

A manufacturing company wants to capture real-time telemetry data from its various equipment and machinery and then analyze the relationships between these data points.

12. Which Azure Cosmos DB API would be the best fit for analyzing relationships in real-time data?

A. Core (SQL) API

B. MongoDB API

C. Gremlin (Graph) API

D. Cassandra API

Your enterprise plans to store confidential documents in Azure. It requires a storage solution that supports both on-premises and Azure-based SMB clients.

13. What would be the most appropriate Azure Storage solution for this need?

A. Azure Data Lake Storage Gen2

B. Azure Blob storage

C. Azure Cosmos DB

D. Azure File storage

A healthcare application is being built that needs to fetch patient information rapidly, no matter where the request comes from, be it Asia, Europe, or the Americas.

14. Which feature of Azure Cosmos DB ensures data is quickly accessible globally?

A. Turnkey global distribution

B. Automatic multiregion writes

C. Geo-replication

D. Locally redundant storage

An e-commerce platform is facing difficulties in managing its rapidly changing inventory. The company is looking for a database that can scale out easily to accommodate spikes in traffic, especially during sales.

15. What feature of Azure Cosmos DB will help manage the rapid changing and scaling needs of the platform?

A. Partitioning

B. Auto-scale throughput

C. Time to live (TTL) settings

D. Geo-fencing

Thought experiment answers

This section contains the answers to the thought experiment. Each answer is explained to give you insights into why that answer was selected.

1. **D** Azure Blob storage

   Explanation: Azure Blob storage is designed for storing large volumes of unstructured data, like videos. It provides cost-effective storage options and can handle the high data throughput required for video streaming.

2. **D** Azure File storage

   Explanation: Azure File storage offers managed file shares for cloud or on-premises deployments. It can integrate with Azure Active Directory and supports SMB, making it suitable as a replacement for traditional shared drives.

3. **B** Azure Cosmos

   Explanation: Azure Cosmos DB is a globally distributed database service that provides low-latency access to data, regardless of where the user is located. Its multiregion replication ensures that data remains highly available.

4. **C** Gremlin (Graph) API

   Explanation: For graph-based analytics, the Gremlin API is most appropriate. It's a graph traversal language and is designed specifically for representing interconnected datasets.

5. **D** Archive

   Explanation: The Archive tier in Azure Blob storage is optimized for storing rarely accessed datasets at a lower cost. It's ideal for data that needs to be retained over long periods without frequent access, such as logs and old telemetry data.

6. **B** Azure Table storage

   Explanation: Azure Table storage is designed to store structured, non-relational data in a key-value format, making it an ideal choice for the firm's transaction records.

7. **D** Azure File storage

   Explanation: Azure File storage provides shared storage for applications using the standard SMB protocol. It can be mounted to VMs, making it a suitable choice for direct access to media files.

8. **B** Azure Cosmos DB

   Explanation: Azure Cosmos DB is designed to provide low latency for both read and write operations, making it ideal for scenarios that require rapid data access.

9. **C** Azure Data Lake Storage Gen2

   Explanation: Azure Data Lake Storage Gen2 offers a hierarchical file system, optimized for big data analytics and AI workloads. It is specifically tailored for the needs of a research organization dealing with large datasets.

10. **B** Azure Cosmos DB with auto-scale throughput

    Explanation: Auto-scale throughput in Azure Cosmos DB adjusts automatically and instantly based on the current workload. This ensures that the e-commerce platform pays only for the throughput they need.

11. **B** Cool

    Explanation: The Cool tier of Azure Blob storage is optimized for storing data that is infrequently accessed and stored for at least 30 days. This makes it suitable for the described logging scenario where older logs are accessed less frequently than the newest ones.

12. **C** Gremlin (Graph) API

    Explanation: The Gremlin (Graph) API is tailored for graph databases that excel at representing and analyzing interconnected data points, making it ideal for examining relationships in real-time data.

13. **D** Azure File storage

    Explanation: Azure File storage provides shared storage using the standard SMB protocol, which supports both on-premises and Azure-based SMB client, ensuring seamless integration.

14. **A** Turnkey Global Distribution

    Turnkey Global Distribution in Azure Cosmos DB ensures that data is available in close proximity to all users worldwide, ensuring low-latency access regardless of the user's geographic location.

15. **B** Auto-scale throughput

Explanation: Azure Cosmos DB allows for automatic and instant scalability based on the current workload, ensuring the platform can handle traffic spikes, especially during high-demand periods such as sales.

These scenarios and questions encourage you to think critically about Azure Storage solutions in a real-world context.

Scenario Exercise

Global Health Tech Corp (GHTC), a health tech company, is looking to set up its new telehealth application on Azure. This application will store patient records, real-time medical data from wearables, uploaded diagnostic files like X-rays, and chat transcripts between doctors and patients. Additionally, it's planning to offer its services across the globe, aiming for low latency, irrespective of the patient or doctor's location.

Your tasks are as follows:

1. Set up Blob storage for diagnostic files:

   ■ Create a Blob storage account suitable for storing X-ray images and other diagnostic files.

   ■ Implement a policy to move these files to a cheaper access tier if they haven't been accessed for more than 30 days.

2. Design Azure File storage for chat transcripts:

   ■ Establish Azure File storage where real-time chat transcripts between doctors and patients will be stored.

   ■ Ensure this storage solution can be accessed both on-premises and on Azure.

3. Design Table storage for wearable data:

   ■ Create an Azure Table storage solution to store structured data coming in from wearables such as heart rate, steps walked, sleep patterns, etc.

   ■ Make sure to design the storage so that it can handle high volumes of incoming data without affecting performance.

4. Set up global distribution with Cosmos DB:

   ■ Design a Cosmos DB database to store patient records.

   ■ Ensure this data is easily and quickly accessible from anywhere in the world.

   ■ Pick the most appropriate Cosmos DB API for a mobile application the company is planning to launch.

5. Offer feedback and recommendations:

   ■ After setting up the previous elements, provide feedback on potential improvements.

   ■ Highlight any security concerns or best practices they should consider.

Here are the submission requirements:

- Once you've completed your tasks, submit a comprehensive document detailing the steps you've taken, with screenshots, to showcase your work. Also, include your feedback and recommendations.

The following exercise immerses you in a real-world situation and requires a hands-on application of the Chapter 3 concepts, ensuring a deeper understanding of the material.

Exercise: Setting Up Azure Services for GHTC's Telehealth Application

The following instructions provide a step-by-step guide to setting up the required services for GHTC's application, offering hands-on experience in configuring Azure services.

1. Set up Blob storage for diagnostic files.

   a. Navigate to the Azure portal.

   b. Click Create a resource > Storage > Storage account, as shown in Figure 3-17.

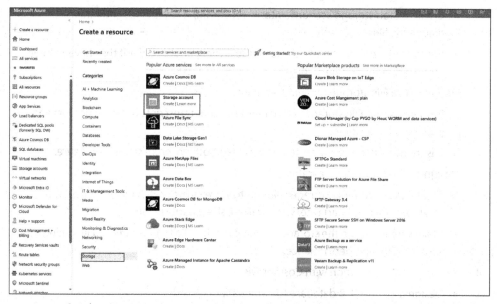

FIGURE 3-17 Creating a storage account

   c. Fill in the required fields, as shown in Figure 3-18.

   - Subscription: Choose your subscription.
   - Resource Group: Create a new resource group or select an existing one.
   - Storage Account Name: Give it a unique name.

- Location: Select a region close to your main user base.
- Performance: Choose Standard.
- Replication: Choose Geo-redundant storage (GRS).

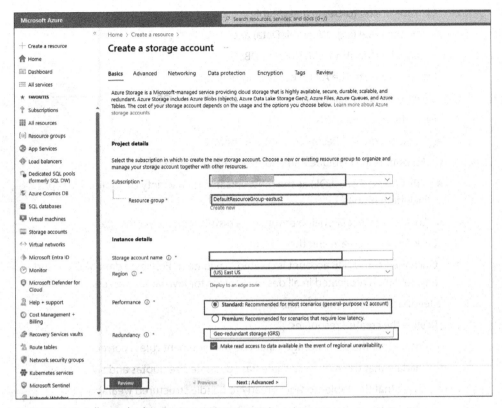

FIGURE 3-18 Details required to create a storage account

    d.   Click Review + create and then Create.

    e.   Navigate to the Lifecycle Management tab under Blob Service in the storage account.

    f.   Create a new rule to move blobs to the Cool tier after 30 days of no access.

2.   Design Azure File storage for chat transcripts.

    a.   Navigate to the previously created storage account.

    b.   Under File Service, select Files.

    c.   Click the + icon to create a new file share.

    d.   Enter a name for your share and an initial quota (size limits).

    e.   Click Create.

    f.   Under Settings > Configuration, ensure the SMB protocol is turned on for your required version.

3. Set up Table storage for wearable data.

   a. Go back to the main page of your storage account.

   b. Under Table Service, select Tables.

   c. Click the + icon to create a new table.

   d. Name the table (e.g., WearableData) and click OK.

4. Set up global distribution with Cosmos DB.

   a. Navigate back to the Azure portal's home page.

   b. Click Create a resource > Databases> Azure Cosmos DB.

   c. Fill in the required fields:

      ■ Subscription and Resource Group: As before.

      ■ Account Name: Unique name for the Cosmos DB account.

      ■ API: Choose Core (SQL) as the most versatile for a variety of application types including mobile.

      ■ Location: Select Global to ensure data distribution across the globe.

   d. Click Review + create and then Create.

   e. Once the Cosmos DB account is created, navigate to Replicate data globally and ensure data is replicated in all desired regions for low-latency access.

5. Give feedback and recommendations.

   a. Review the created resources:

      ■ Ensure that the Blob storage's lifecycle management rule is correctly set.

      ■ Validate that the Azure File share has adequate size quotas and SMB access.

      ■ Check that the Table storage is ready to handle structured wearable data.

      ■ Confirm the global replication settings in Cosmos DB.

   b. Make security recommendations.

      ■ Recommend using Azure RBAC for controlling access to resources.

      ■ Advise on setting up network security groups and virtual networking service endpoints to secure connections.

   c. Submit feedback.

      ■ Document all the steps taken with accompanying screenshots.

      ■ Include potential areas of improvement and security recommendations.

CHAPTER 4

Describe an analytics workload on Azure

In this chapter, you are embarking on a journey into analytics workloads on Azure—a domain that serves as the nerve center for data-driven decision-making in today's complex business environment. This chapter furnishes you with essential knowledge and skills in three distinct, yet interconnected, areas of analytics.

First, we'll demystify the realm of large-scale analytics. You'll come to understand the multifaceted nature of data ingestion and its foundational processing elements that can make or break your analytics pipeline. Moreover, we'll delve into the concepts of analytical data stores and their significance in storing and retrieving large volumes of data efficiently. With a myriad of Azure services available for data warehousing, you'll learn how to navigate this landscape and select solutions that best align with your specific requirements.

Second, we transition into the fast-paced world of real-time data analytics. With the acceleration of data generation and the increasing need for immediate insights, mastering real-time analytics is more vital than ever. This section will provide a nuanced understanding of both batch and streaming data, offering insights into when and how to utilize each for optimal results. In addition, you'll be introduced to Azure's specialized technologies that make real-time analytics not just possible but efficient and scalable.

Finally, we will tackle the art and science of data visualization using Microsoft Power BI. Power BI is a powerful tool in your analytics arsenal, and with it you can transform raw data into compelling visual narratives. You'll get an in-depth look at the capabilities of Power BI, from its robust data modeling features to its various options for data visualization. By the end of this section, you'll be well-equipped to convey complex data stories in an easily digestible format.

This chapter promises to be a comprehensive guide to effectively navigating the intricacies of Azure analytics workloads. With these skills, you'll be better prepared to handle the challenges and opportunities that come with managing and interpreting data on a large scale.

Skills covered in this chapter:

- Skill 4.1 Describe common elements of large-scale analytics
- Skill 4.2 Describe consideration for real-time data analytics
- Skill 4.3 Describe data visualization in Microsoft Power BI

Skill 4.1 Describe common elements of large-scale analytics

In this section, we will delve into the pivotal components of large-scale analytics, a cornerstone for any data-intensive operation. At its core, this skill underscores the necessity to understand data ingestion and its consequential processing. Grasping these topics can dramatically shape the efficiency and accuracy of your analytics workflow. Furthermore, you'll be introduced to the concepts of the analytical data store, a hub that facilitates vast data storage and retrieval. And as we navigate this vast landscape, we'll also highlight specific Azure services tailored for data warehousing so you can choose the best tools for your analytics requirements. In essence, this section equips you with the foundational knowledge to orchestrate seamless, large-scale analytics operations on Azure.

> **This skill covers how to:**
> - Describe large-scale data warehousing architecture
> - Describe considerations for data ingestion and processing
> - Describe options for analytical data stores
> - Describe Azure services for data warehousing

Describe large-scale data warehousing architecture

Large-scale data warehousing is an evolution from traditional data warehouses, engineered to handle enormous datasets, diverse data sources, and complex analytical requirements typical of big enterprises or global operations. The architecture for such scale must be robust, flexible, and highly optimized for performance. Let's explore this architectural landscape.

Components of Azure's large-scale data warehousing architecture

The architecture encompasses the following:

- **Azure data sources:** Dive into various Azure services such as Azure SQL Database, Azure Cosmos DB, and Azure Blob Storage. Each caters to specific data needs and scenarios.

- **Azure Data Factory:** Think of this as your control center. With this cloud-based integration service, you can orchestrate and automate data movements and transformations seamlessly.

- **Azure Synapse Analytics:** A high-performance warehouse, Synapse is tailored to crunch vast datasets, offering you the flexibility to query data on-demand or use provisioned resources.

- **Azure Analysis Services:** This service is a highly scalable and fully managed platform for complex data exploration and transformation. It enables the construction of advanced semantic models, providing a robust framework for multidimensional analytics that translates intricate datasets into actionable insights.
- **Visualization with Power BI and Azure Data Share:** These tools will be your final pit stops. Use them to visualize, share, and make sense of the wealth of information residing in your data warehouse.

Crafting architectures in the Azure landscape

Azure isn't just about tools; it's about crafting solutions:

- **Two-tier and three-tier frameworks:** Azure champions modularity. Whether you're looking at a two-tier or a more comprehensive three-tier setup, focus on modularization, decoupling, and scalability.
- **Synapse's serverless and provisioned models:** With Azure Synapse Analytics, you get to choose between on-demand (serverless) or provisioned resources, ensuring you have optimal performance for your workload without overcommitting resources.

The Azure advantage

These are the advantages of Azure:

- **Seamless interplay:** One of Azure's strengths is the seamless integration between its services. This ensures a fluid data journey, from source to insights.
- **Safety first:** Your data's security is paramount. With Azure, benefit from its built-in security and compliance features, ensuring peace of mind even with massive datasets.
- **Adaptable and scalable:** The Azure landscape morphs with your needs. Take advantage of its flexibility, scaling resources as your data needs evolve.

Practical scenario

Let's immerse ourselves in a scenario where you play the role of a chief data officer for an international retailer named GlobaRetail Inc.

Figure 4-1 shows the key data journey components that are crucial to this scenario.

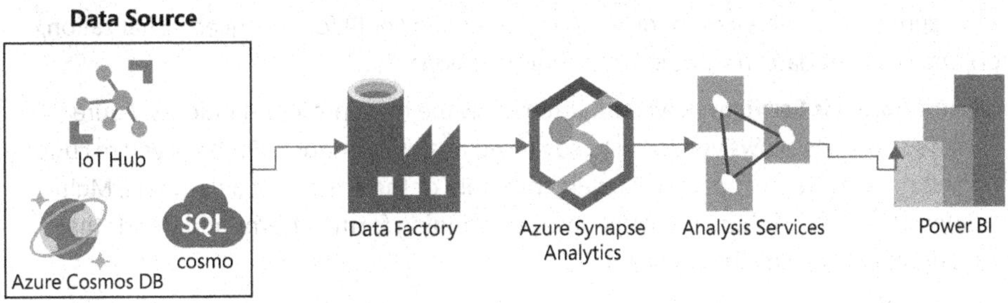

FIGURE 4-1 Data journey from Azure data sources to visualization to Power BI

SETTING THE STAGE

As the chief data officer at GlobaRetail Inc., you oversee the expansive operations, so you need to leverage cutting-edge Azure services to effectively manage your vast data landscape. You have the following options:

- **Azure SQL Database:** Your stores across 40 countries register millions of transactions daily. Each transaction, from purchase to return, is meticulously logged in Azure SQL Database. This platform not only offers scalability to handle the data but ensures consistent performance across peak shopping periods.

- **Azure Cosmos DB:** Your product range is vast and diversified, catering to global tastes. Azure Cosmos DB becomes your go-to solution, hosting the dynamic product catalog with its globally distributed setup. This ensures that product details, price adjustments, and stock levels are consistently and quickly accessible, regardless of where a customer is shopping from.

- **IoT Hub:** In modern store operations, sensors are deployed across outlets. They track customer footfalls, monitor shelf stocks, and even regulate store lighting and temperature. The real-time stream of data from these sensors funnels through Azure's IoT Hub.

DATA TRANSFORMATION AND ANALYTICS

Navigating the intricacies of data transformation and analytics is central to your role. You can utilize Azure Data Factory and Azure Synapse Analytics to streamline and enrich the decision-making process:

- **Azure Data Factory:** With such diverse data sources, integration can be challenging. Using Azure Data Factory, you define and orchestrate data-driven workflows. Data from Azure SQL Database, Cosmos DB, and IoT Hub is routinely cleaned, validated, and merged. Seasonal promotions, for instance, can be analyzed by correlating sales data with footfall patterns.

- **Azure Synapse Analytics:** After integration, data is channeled to Azure Synapse Analytics. Here, large-scale analytical computations occur. Analysts can query to understand patterns, such as to find out if a certain store layout drives more sales or if weather impacts shopping behavior in specific regions.

DEEP ANALYTICS AND VISUALIZATION

Leverage Azure Analysis Services for deep analytics and Power BI for advanced visualization, transforming complex data insights into strategic decisions:

- **Azure Analysis Services:** Raw data often hides the most profound insights. Azure Analysis Services allows you to build advanced analytical models. Perhaps you're curious about the long-term impact of a loyalty program or the efficacy of a flash sale. Multidimensional analysis here can offer answers, bringing forth patterns and trends that might otherwise remain obscured.

- **Power BI:** With insights at hand, the final task is to make them digestible and action-able. Power BI creates dashboards to visually represent data stories. Maybe there's a heat map showcasing global sales hotspots or a line chart tracing the spike in sales during holiday seasons. It's not just about numbers; it's about pairing the data with a picture that drives business strategy.

Guided by the insights derived from this intricate data journey, GlobaRetail Inc. tweaks its marketing campaigns, optimizes store layouts, adjusts inventory level, and even plans its expansion strategy into new markets.

By understanding and harnessing these Azure capabilities, you, as the decision-maker, are not just reacting to the market; you're proactively steering your company based on a founda-tion of solid data-driven insights.

NEED MORE REVIEW? **LARGE-SCALE DATA WAREHOUSING**

You can learn more about large-scale data warehousing at *learn.microsoft.com/en-us/azure/ architecture/example-scenario/data/data-warehouse*.

Describe considerations for data ingestion and processing

Data ingestion and processing, two core stages of the data lifecycle, are paramount when orchestrating analytics solutions, especially in cloud ecosystems like Azure. As data flows from its origin to its destination, it often undergoes multiple transformations, making the consid-erations for ingesting and processing crucial for accuracy, efficiency, and scalability. In this extensive overview, we'll unpack these considerations, delving deeper into the world of data pipelines, transformation mechanisms, and the choices Azure offers.

- **Understanding data sources:** Every analytics solution starts with understanding where your data originates.
  - **Type of data:** Data can be structured (like SQL databases), semi-structured (like JSON or XML files), or unstructured (like logs or images). Each type may require dif-ferent ingestion tools and techniques.
  - **Integration with Azure:** Azure provides a plethora of connectors and integration solutions. Azure Synapse, for instance, has connectors for databases, data lakes, on-premises data sources, and many third-party services.

    For example, suppose your primary data source is a set of IoT devices. These devices generate high-velocity streaming data, which is often semi-structured.

    Figure 4-2 shows some data types.

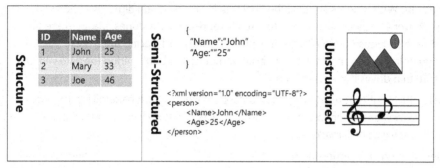

FIGURE 4-2 Data types

- **Data volume, velocity, and variety:** These three Vs dictate your data strategy.
  - **Volume:** This refers to the amount of data you handle. Whether you're dealing with gigabytes or petabytes will influence your storage and processing choices.
  - **Velocity:** This is the rate at which new data is generated and ingested into your system. This could range from real-time data streams to infrequent batch uploads.
  - **Variety:** As previously mentioned, data can come in many formats. The diversity of your data sources can affect your ingestion and processing methods.
- **Data pipelines, the heart of data movement:** In the Azure ecosystem, a data pipeline is the orchestrated flow of data from its source to its destination. Azure Synapse and Azure Data Factory are the primary services designed for this, allowing you to design and manage these pipelines.
  - **Pipeline activities:** These are the actions or "tasks" within a pipeline, like copying data running a data processing activity or executing a data flow.
  - **Triggers:** These define the conditions under which a pipeline runs. They could be scheduled or event-driven.

    For example, a retail company might set up a pipeline in Azure Data Factory or Azure Synapse to ingest sales data at the end of every business day, transforming and aggregating this data for daily sales reports. Figure 4-3 depicts the Azure Data Factory Pipeline workflow.

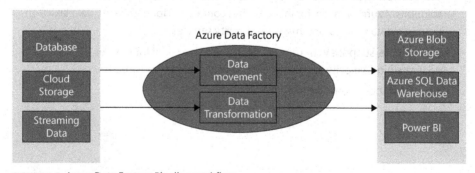

FIGURE 4-3 Azure Data Factory Pipeline workflow

- **Transformations such as ETL versus ELT:** Depending on when you transform your data (before or after loading it into your analytical store), you might be working with extract, transform, load (ETL) or extract, load, transform (ELT). See Figure 4-4.

  - **ETL:** ETL is best when raw data needs cleaning or transformation before it's suitable for analytical processing.

  - **ELT:** ELT is suitable when the analytical data store in powerful enough to handle transformations. Azure's Synapse Analytics (formerly SQL Data Warehouse) is designed for this approach.

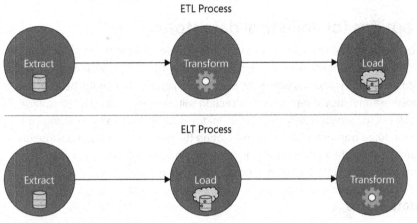

FIGURE 4-4 ETL versus ELT

- **Security, compliance, and data governance:** Azure provides a comprehensive suite of tools and best practices to ensure your data is secure and compliant.

  - **Encryption:** Always ensure data is encrypted both in transit and at rest. Services like Azure Blob Storage provide automatic encryption.

  - **Access control:** Use Azure Active Directory for identity services and role-based access control.

  - **Auditing and monitoring:** Regularly monitor data operations using tools like Azure Monitor and Log Analytics.

- **Scalability, reliability, and cost management:** Azure's cloud-based model allows for immense scalability, but it's essential to manage resources effectively.

  - **Scaling:** Use services that allow both vertical and horizontal scaling. Azure Cosmos DB, for instance, provides global distribution and elastic scaling of throughput.

  - **Reliability:** Ensure your services have redundancy and backup capabilities. Azure's geo-redundant storage (GRS) is a good example of a service that provides auto-mated backups in multiple locations.

  - **Cost management:** Monitor and analyze your Azure spending with tools such as Azure Cost Management and Azure Advisor.

As you venture deeper into Azure's world of data ingestion and processing, it's paramount to approach the subject with a holistic view. By focusing on these critical considerations, you'll ensure that your data solutions are not only efficient but also secure, scalable, and cost-effective.

> **NEED MORE REVIEW?** **DATA PIPELINE**
>
> You can learn more about Azure Data Pipeline at *learn.microsoft.com/en-us/azure/ data-factory/introduction*.

Describe options for analytical data stores

In the digital age, data has been likened to oil, a valuable resource driving the engines of modern businesses. But raw data, much like unrefined oil, has limited use. The transformation of this raw material into actionable insights is where the true magic happens, and at the heart of this alchemical process are analytical data stores. This section will cover these specialized storage systems, each tailored to harness data's potential in unique ways. Whether you're diving into vast oceans of structured transactional data or navigating the nebulous realms of unstructured social media content, the right analytical data store not only holds the key but also maps the path to treasures of insights. Let's discover the possibilities they present.

Relational data stores

Relational data stores are the backbone of structured data storage. Designed around tables with predefined schemas, they shine when you're working with structured datasets and need to run intricate queries.

For example, think of an e-commerce store's transactional data. Each purchase, customer detail, and product attribute fits neatly into tables that relate to each other, as shown in Table 4-1.

TABLE 4-1 Relational data stores

Customer ID	Product ID	Transaction amount (in USD)
1001	P5678	$150.00
1002	P5679	$45.00
1002	P5680	$99.99
1003	P5678	$150.00
1002	P5681	$60.00
1004	P5679	$45.00
1005	P5682	$210.00

Table 4-1 illustrates a simple relational database structure. Each row represents a unique transaction. The same customer (like Customer ID 1001) can make multiple transactions and purchase different products. The Transaction Amount column denotes the cost of each product during the transaction.

NoSQL Data Store

Stepping away from strict relational schemas, NoSQL offers flexibility. NoSQL data stores are ideal for semi-structured or unstructured data, including documents, key-values, and more. Figure 4-5 demonstrates the flexibility offered by NoSQL with varying data points.

For example, consider social media posts. Each post might have varied data points; some might have images, and others might have polls or videos. NoSQL handles this variability gracefully.

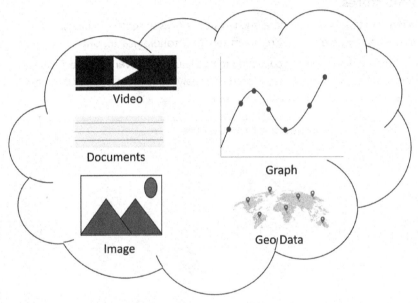

FIGURE 4-5 Data points supported by NoSQL

Columnar data stores

Designed for analytics, columnar data stores organize data in columns rather than rows. This makes aggregations and analytics blazing fast, as reading becomes more efficient for analytical queries.

For example, imagine a scenario where you're analyzing sales trends based on product colors across millions of entries. Rather than scanning rows, columnar stores read the color column efficiently, as shown in Figure 4-6.

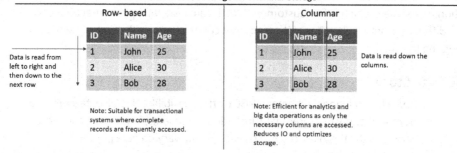

FIGURE 4-6 Row-based versus columnar storage

Time-series data stores

When you're dealing with time-stamped data, such as stock prices or sensor readings, time-series databases come into play. They're optimized for chronological insights.

For example, picture a weather station collecting temperature data every minute. Over months, this becomes a massive dataset, best stored and analyzed via a time-series database. Figure 4-7 shows temperature data collected over a week.

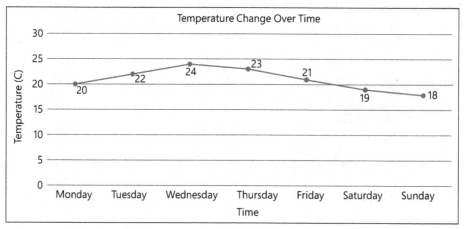

FIGURE 4-7 Time-series data store

When you dive into Azure's analytical ecosystem, you'll encounter two standout data stores tailor-made for your analytics needs: Azure Synapse Analytics and Azure Data Lake Storage Gen2.

With Azure Synapse Analytics, previously known as Azure SQL Data Warehouse, you get a compilation of big data warehousing capabilities. This platform allows you to swiftly scale resources up or down, paying only for what you use. An integrated workspace in Synapse Analytics offers you a singular experience, blending big data and data warehousing. Whether your workload demands on-demand query processing or provisioned resources, Synapse Analytics accommodates both. What's more, Synapse Studio lets you explore your data on the fly, without the hassle of infrastructure setups.

Azure Data Lake Storage Gen2 is a vast, scalable, and secure data lake optimized for big data analytics. The unique aspect of this store is its hierarchical namespace, which combines the prowess of Azure Blob Storage with a structured file system, thereby boosting analytics performance. Security is paramount here. Integration with Azure Active Directory, combined with POSIX-compliant access controls, ensures your data's sanctity. To top it off, tools like Azure Data Factory come to your aid for seamless data movement, making it easier for you to integrate with other Azure data services such as Azure Databricks or Azure HDInsight.

Describe Azure services for data warehousing

As you embark on the exhilarating path of data warehousing with Azure, it's like standing at the helm of a vast ocean of possibilities. Azure's suite of service offers you not just tools but a palette of choices, each unique, powerful, and designed to cater to the complex tapestry of modern data needs. Within this realm, there are luminaries such as Azure Synapse analytics, Azure Databricks, Azure HDInsight, Microsoft Fabric, and Azure Data Factory. Each represents a different shade of Azure Analytical prowess, promising to transform raw data into insight, numbers into narratives, and questions into actionable strategies. Let's set sail and navigate through these pivotal services, illuminating your path to masterful data orchestration and analytics.

Azure Synapse Analytics

Figure 4-8 shows the logo used to represent Azure Synapse Analytics globally.

FIGURE 4-8 Azure Synapse logo

Formerly known as Azure SQL Data Warehouse, Azure Synapse Analytics offers a blend of enterprise data warehousing and big data analytics. Imagine you have a vast pool of structured and unstructured data that you want to analyze quickly. Azure Synapse Analytics lets you manage, analyze, and visualize such datasets in real time.

Azure Databricks

Figure 4-9 shows the logo used to represent Azure Databricks globally.

FIGURE 4-9 Azure Databricks logo

Dive into Spark-based analytics with Azure Databricks. It's a collaborative Apache Spark–based analytics platform optimized for Azure, providing you with streamlined workflows and an interactive workspace. Let's say you're working on a machine learning project that requires vast amounts of data processing and collaboration. With Databricks, you and your team can work seamlessly on notebooks, scale resources on-demand, and integrate with various Azure services to build end-to-end solutions.

Azure HDInsight

Figure 4-10 shows the logo used to represent Azure HDInsight globally.

FIGURE 4-10 Azure HDInsight logo

Venture into the world of open-source analytics with Azure HDInsight. It's a cloud service that brings to your fingertips leading open-source frameworks such as Hadoop, Spark, Hive, and more. Imagine wanting to process log files spread across a decade to extract patterns. HDInsight, with its scalable clusters, can process these logs efficiently and provide actionable insights.

Azure Data Factory

Figure 4-11 shows the logo used to represent Azure Data Factory globally.

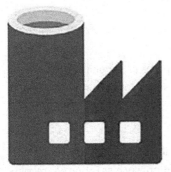

FIGURE 4-11 Azure Data Factory logo

Your data often resides in diverse locations, formats, and structures. Azure Data Factory is your go-to orchestration tool to collect and move data across various supported Azure data stores. Think of it as the bridge connecting your data sources to your analytics engines. If you have sales data in on-premises SQL databases and want to merge it with clickstream data in a blob store for warehousing, Data Factory can orchestrate that flow seamlessly.

Azure Data Factory

Figure 4-12 shows all the components of Microsoft Fabric.

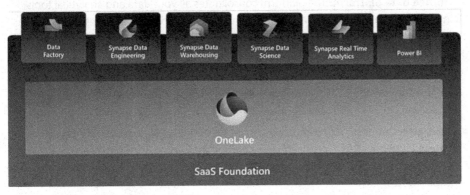

FIGURE 4-12 Microsoft Fabric components

Microsoft Fabric is an integrated analytics platform that combines data warehousing, data engineering, data science, and business intelligence into a single, unified experience. It's built on a software-as-a-service (SaaS) foundation, bringing together existing components from Power BI, Azure Synapse Analytics, and Azure Data Factory. This eliminates the need to stitch together different services from various vendors and simplifies your analytics needs.

DATAWAREHOUSE IN MICROSOFT FABRIC

Fabric offers two distinct data warehousing experiences:

- **SQL Analytics endpoint of the lakehouse:** This is an automatically generated warehouse created from your lakehouse in Microsoft Fabric. It provides a familiar SQL interface for data analysts and business users to query and analyze data without needing to learn new tools or languages.

- **Warehouse:** The warehouse is a dedicated data store optimized for analytical workloads. It offers greater flexibility and control over data management compared to the SQL analytics endpoint. You can define schemas, create tables and views, and manage partitions and indexes.

BENEFITS OF USING MICROSOFT FABRIC FOR DATA WAREHOUSING:

In the realm of data warehousing, the advent of innovative solutions such as Fabric has revolutionized how businesses manage, process, and analyze their data. Fabric is a game-changing platform, offering a suite of features that streamline and optimize the data warehousing process. Its capabilities extend beyond traditional data management methodologies, providing a unified, scalable, and cost-effective approach to handling vast datasets. Here's a closer look at the key benefits of using Fabric for your data warehouse:

- **Simplified data management:** Fabric's ease of use in data ingestion, transformation, and loading is a significant advantage. It offers an array of prebuilt connectors, intuitive drag-and-drop data flows, and flexible code-based transformations, which simplify the traditionally complex processes of data integration and manipulation.

- **Unified data platform:** The platform consolidates all your data and analytical tools into a single, cohesive environment. This unification not only streamlines operations but also fosters collaboration and easier sharing of insights across teams.

- **Scalability and elasticity:** One of Fabric's core strengths lies in its ability to adapt to your evolving data needs. Whether you are scaling up to accommodate growing data volumes or scaling down during quieter periods, Fabric ensures that your data warehouse can flexibly meet your business demands.

- **Cost-effectiveness:** With Fabric, you're not only investing in a powerful data warehousing tool but also in a cost-efficient solution. Its flexible pricing models are designed to align with various budgetary requirements, making it a viable option for a wide range of businesses.

The best Azure data warehousing service for you will depend on your specific requirements. Consider factors such as your data volume, budget, and desired level of control. If you're looking for a simple and easy-to-use solution, Microsoft Fabric is a great option. For more complex and demanding workloads, Azure Synapse Analytics may be a better choice.

As you immerse yourself into Azure's data warehousing services, you'll notice each one's unique strengths and how they can collaborate. For a deeper dive and to ensure you're updated with the latest capabilities, you may want to check the official Azure documentation.

This will not only bolster your foundational understanding but also provide you with practical steps and best practices as you venture forth in your data journey.

NEED MORE REVIEW? **ANALYTICAL DATA STORES**

You can learn more about analytical data stores at *learn.microsoft.com/en-us/training/ modules/examine-components-of-modern-data-warehouse/4-analytical-data-stores*.

Skill 4.2 Describe consideration for real-time data analytics

Imagine you're monitoring a mission-critical system for your organization. A sudden spike in user activity or an unexpected system error could have significant consequences. How swiftly would you want insights into such events? Waiting for end-of-day reports or even hourly summaries won't cut it. You'd want information immediately, as events unfold. This is where real-time data analytics come into play.

In the realm of data, not everything waits for periodic batch processing, especially in today's digital age. The need to make quick decisions based on real-time data is becoming increasingly essential. Whether you're tracking inventory levels in a fast-paced e-commerce environment, monitoring health metrics in a critical-care unit, or gauging customer sentiment on a trending social media hashtag, the sooner you have the data insights, the faster you can act.

Dive into this section to grasp the importance and considerations of real-time analytics. You'll learn about the distinction between batch and streaming data and the pivotal role they play. While batch data gives you a historical context, streaming data is your window to the "now," and understanding the dynamics between the two is crucial.

Consider the intricate dance of city traffic, as illustrated in Figure 4-13. Just as traffic signals and sensors adjust to the ebb and flow of vehicles and direct them efficiently in real time, your analytical systems should be designed to capture, process, and react to the continuous stream of data, providing insights at the speed of your business operations.

FIGURE 4-13 Traffic light signal

Consider an e-commerce platform during a Black Friday sale. With thousands of transactions per minute, the inventory system must update in real time. Outdated information could lead to overselling a product that's already out of stock. By leveraging technologies designed for real-time analytics, the platform can instantly adjust product availability, send alerts, and even direct advertising content based on inventory status. Real-time analytics is a game-changer that ensures smooth operations and enhances the customer experience.

As you delve deeper into this chapter, remember that the world of real-time analytics is not just about speed; it's about timely insights that empower decision-making. Tools and platforms like Azure Stream Analytics and Azure Databricks are your allies in this journey. Harnessing them effectively will let you navigate the fast-paced currents of data and stay competitive.

This skill covers how to:
- Describe the difference between batch and streaming data
- Identify Microsoft cloud services for real-time analytics

Describe the difference between batch and streaming data

When navigating the intricate world of data analytics, you'll often encounter two primary modes of data processing: batch and streaming. To harness the power of your data, understanding the distinction between these two is crucial.

Batch data

At its core, batch processing is about dealing with data in large chunks or batches. Imagine you've been on a trip and taken numerous photos. At the end of the day, you transfer all these photos at once to your computer. That's batch processing. In data analytics, batch processing means you're accumulating data over a specific period and then processing it all at once. This approach is ideal when dealing with vast volumes of data that don't require immediate analysis. For example, if you're analyzing monthly sales data, you'd typically wait for the month to end, collect all the sales records, and then process them together, as shown in Figure 4-14.

Here are the characteristics of batch data:

- **Volume-driven:** Batch processing typically handles enormous volumes of data. It's designed for efficiency and can process vast datasets at optimized costs.
- **Scheduled:** Operations in batch processing are often pre-scheduled, occurring at fixed times like the end of the day or the end of the week.
- **Latency:** Since data is processed after accumulation, there's inherent latency in obtaining insights from batch data.

Here are the challenges of batch data:

- **Data freshness:** As data isn't processed immediately upon arrival, insights might not reflect the most current state of affairs.

- **Resource management:** Handling the surge of processing needs when dealing with large batches requires optimal resource allocation.

FIGURE 4-14 Time-series data store

Streaming data

Now, imagine you're watching a live broadcast of a sports event, and every moment is being captured and transmitted to your screen instantly. This immediacy is the essence of streaming data. In the realm of data analytics, streaming (often referred to as *real-time processing*) involves continuously capturing and analyzing data as it's generated. Let's say you're monitoring the heartbeat of a patient in a hospital. Every heartbeat is vital information that needs immediate attention. In such cases, waiting to collect data over time isn't an option; you analyze it as it comes.

Here are the characteristics of streaming data:

- **Event-driven:** Unlike batch processing, which waits for a volume threshold, streaming processes data point by point as events occur.
- **Low latency:** Streaming data delivers insights with minimal delay, often in milliseconds.
- **Continuous monitoring:** Streaming data systems are always "on," awaiting incoming data.

Here are the challenges of streaming data:

- **Infrastructure needs:** Real-time processing requires a robust infrastructure to handle the constant influx of data.
- **Data volume:** While individual data points are processed swiftly, managing the sheer volume of streaming data can be challenging.

Figure 4-15 illustrates the concept of streaming data.

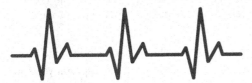

FIGURE 4-15 Streaming data

To give you another relatable example, think of batch processing as reading a book chapter by chapter, where you absorb and reflect on each chapter before moving to the next. In contrast, streaming data is akin to a live conversation, where you're listening, processing, and responding in real time.

The difference between batch and streaming data isn't just technical; it influences business decisions, operational efficiency, and customer experience. Suppose you're running an e-commerce platform. Batch data might help you understand monthly sales trends, but when a high-profile customer faces transaction issues, you need real-time analytics to intervene promptly.

As you dive deeper into these domains, consider your organization's specific needs. Are you aiming for a comprehensive understanding of vast datasets, or do you need pulse-like real-time insights? Often, the most robust data strategies employ a harmonious blend of both.

Remember, the tools and platforms available, especially in Azure's arsenal, are designed to cater to these nuances. Mastering when each is applicable can be a game-changer in your data analytics journey.

> **NEED MORE REVIEW?** **CHOOSING AN ANALYTICS SOLUTION**
>
> You can learn more about analytic solutions at *learn.microsoft.com/en-us/azure/architecture/data-guide/technology-choices/batch-processing*.

Identify Microsoft cloud services for real-time analytics

In an age where decisions must often be made at the blink of an eye, the role of real-time analytics has become paramount. The ability to rapidly sift through vast streams of data, distill meaningful insights, and act on them instantaneously can often mean the difference between seizing an opportunity or missing it entirely. But beyond the buzzwords, what does *real-time analytics* truly entail, especially when you're navigating the vast offerings of the Azure ecosystem? This section will guide you through Azure's real-time analytics technologies, demystifying their capabilities and applications and setting you on a course to harness their full potential. From understanding the prowess of Azure Stream Analytics to grasping the nuances of Azure Synapse Data Explorer and Spark structured streaming, you're about to get to the heart of instant data processing and analytics.

- **Stream processing platforms:** At the center stage of real-time analytics are stream processing platforms. A stalwart example is Azure Stream Analytics, which you can use to ingest, process, and analyze data as it flows. To visualize its power, consider monitoring a vast power grid, instantly detecting surges, and redirecting power to prevent outages. Just like the grid managers, you can harness Azure Stream Analytics to react immediately to your business's data.

- **Azure Synapse Data Explorer:** This isn't just another tool—it's your window into the massive streams of data you're dealing with. With Azure Synapse Data Explorer you can query, visualize, and explore your data in real time. It's like having a magnifying glass over a rushing river of data, where you can pick out and examine individual drops (or data points) as they flow by.

- **Spark Structured Streaming:** An integral part of the Apache Spark ecosystem, Spark Structured Streaming facilitates scalable and fault-tolerant stream processing of live data streams. Imagine standing amidst a bustling stock market, with traders shouting orders and prices fluctuating wildly. Now, imagine you could process, aggregate, and make sense of all that data in real time. That's the magic Spark Structured Streaming brings to the table. Figure 4-16 shows you streaming lines of data converging into structured blocks of information.

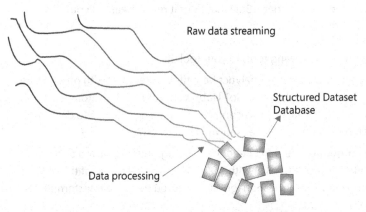

Raw data streaming

Structured Dataset Database

Data processing

FIGURE 4-16 Streaming data converging into structured datasets

- **Message brokers:** Azure Event Hubs stands tall as a premier message broker. As you navigate the labyrinth of real-time data, you'll realize the critical role of these brokers in ensuring data is delivered reliably and promptly to the systems that process them. It's the backbone, the silent carrier ensuring every piece of data reaches its destination.

- **NoSQL databases:** In the realm of real-time data, traditional databases can become bottlenecks. This is where powerhouses like Cosmos DB shine. Designed for breakneck speeds and unmatched scalability, they provide the storage that might be required for the deluge of real-time data. If you've ever wondered how global social media platforms can show trending topics within seconds of an event unfolding, NoSQL databases are a big part of that answer.

- **Data visualization tools:** The journey from data to decision is completed when insights are visualized and made actionable. Power BI serves as a beacon here, integrating with real-time analytics platforms to deliver live data dashboards. These aren't just numbers and graphs; they're the pulse of your operations, showcased in real time.

The ecosystem of real-time analytics is vast and ever-evolving. As you delve deeper, be prepared to witness the symphony of technologies working in unison, each playing its unique note in the grand composition of real-time insights. Each technology, be it Azure Stream Analytics,

Azure Synapse Data Explorer, or Spark Structured Streaming, has its own nuances, applications, and potentials.

Azure Stream Analytics

In today's data-driven world, the need to react immediately to unfolding events has never been greater. Picture yourself on the trading floor, where milliseconds can decide millions. Or consider a bustling metropolis where urban sensors constantly monitor traffic, air quality, and energy consumption. Azure Stream Analytics is Microsoft's answer to the challenges of real-time data ingestion, processing, and analytics.

Azure Stream Analytics is a real-time event data processing service that you can use to harness the power of fast-moving streams of data. But what does it really mean for you?

WHY AZURE STREAM ANALYTICS?

Azure Stream Analytics brings the following tools to your toolkit:

- **Seamless integration:** Azure Stream Analytics beautifully integrates with other Azure services. Whether you're pulling data from IoT Hub, Event Hub, or Blob Storage, Stream Analytics acts as your cohesive layer, processing and redirecting the data to databases, dashboards, or even other applications, as shown in Figure 4-17.

- **SQL-based query language:** You don't need to be a programming wizard to harness Azure Stream Analytics. If you're familiar with SQL, you're already ahead of the curve. Stream Analytics employs a SQL-like language, allowing you to create transformation queries on your real-time data.

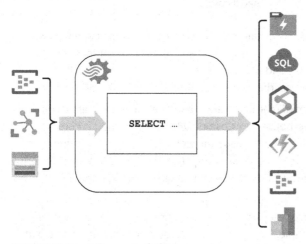

FIGURE 4-17 Azure Stream Analytics

- **Scalability and reliability:** One of the hallmarks of Azure Stream Analytics is its ability to scale. Whether you're processing a few records or millions every second, Stream Analytics can handle it. More so, its built-in recovery capabilities ensure that no data is lost in the case of failures.

- **Real-time dashboards:** Azure Stream Analytics is not just about processing; it's also about visualization. With its ability to integrate seamlessly with tools like Power BI, you can access real-time dashboards that update as events unfold.

- **Time windowing:** One of the stand-out features you'll appreciate is the ease with which you can perform operations over specific time windows—be it tumbling, sliding, or hopping. For instance, you might want to calculate the average temperature from IoT sensors every five minutes; Stream Analytics has got you covered.

  Tumbling window in stream processing refers to a fixed-duration, nonoverlapping interval used to segment time-series data. Each piece of data falls into exactly one window, defined by a distinct start and end time, ensuring that data groups are mutually exclusive. For instance, with a 5-minute tumbling window, data from 00:00 to 00:04 would be aggregated in one window, and data from 00:05 to 00:09 in the next, facilitating structured, periodic analysis of streaming data.

  Sliding window in stream processing is a type of data analysis technique where the window of time for data aggregation "slides" continuously over the data stream. This means that the window moves forward by a specified slide interval, and it overlaps with previous windows. Each window has a fixed length, but unlike tumbling windows, sliding windows can cover overlapping periods of time, allowing for more frequent analysis and updates. For example, if you have a sliding window of 10 minutes with a slide interval of 5 minutes, a new window starts every 5 minutes, and each window overlaps with the previous one for 5 minutes, providing a more continuous and overlapping view of the data stream.

  Hopping window in stream processing is a time-based window that moves forward in fixed increments, known as the hop size. Each window has a specified duration, and the start of the next window is determined by the hop size rather than the end of the previous window. This approach allows for overlaps between windows, where data can be included in multiple consecutive windows if it falls within their time frames. For example, with a window duration of 10 minutes and a hop size of 5 minutes, a new window starts every 5 minutes, and each window overlaps with the next one for a duration determined by the difference between the window size and the hop size.

- **Anomaly detection:** Dive into the built-in machine learning capabilities to detect anomalies in your real-time data streams. Whether you're monitoring web clickstreams or machinery in a factory, Azure Stream Analytics can alert you to significant deviations in patterns.

As a practical example to truly appreciate the potential of Azure Stream Analytics, consider a smart city initiative. Urban sensors, spread across the city, send real-time data about traffic, energy consumption, and more. Through Azure Stream Analytics, this data is ingested in real time, processed to detect any irregularities such as traffic jams or power surges, and then passed on to Power BI dashboards that city officials monitor. The officials can then take immediate action, such as rerouting traffic or adjusting power distribution.

In summary, Azure Stream Analytics is a tool for those yearning to transform raw, real-time data streams into actionable, meaningful insights. And as you delve deeper into its features and integrations, you'll realize that its possibilities are vast and ever-evolving.

Azure Data Explorer

As the digital age progresses, the influx of data has transformed from a steady stream into a roaring torrent. Capturing, analyzing, and acting upon this data in real time is not just a luxury but a necessity for businesses to remain competitive and relevant. Enter Azure Data Explorer, a service uniquely equipped to manage, analyze, and visualize this deluge of information. This section is your comprehensive guide to understanding and harnessing its immense potential.

WHAT IS AZURE DATA EXPLORER?

Azure Data Explorer (ADX) is a fast, fully managed data analytics service for real-time analysis on large volumes of streaming data. It brings together big data and analytics into a unified platform that provides solutions to some of the most complex data exploration challenges.

Here are its key features and benefits:

- **Rapid ingestion and analysis:** One of the hallmarks of Azure Data Explorer is its ability to ingest millions of records per second and simultaneously query across billions of records in mere seconds. Such speed ensures that you're always working with the most recent data.

- **Intuitive query language:** Kusto Query Language (KQL) is the heart of Azure Data Explorer. If you've used SQL, transitioning to KQL will feel familiar. It allows you to write complex ad hoc queries, making data exploration and analysis a breeze.

- **Scalability:** ADX can scale out by distributing data and query load across multiple nodes. This horizontal scaling ensures that as your data grows, your ability to query it remains swift.

- **Integration with other Azure services:** ADX plays nicely with other Azure services, ensuring that you can integrate it seamlessly into your existing data infrastructure. Whether it's ingesting data from Event Hubs, IoT Hub, or a myriad of other sources, ADX can handle it. Figure 4-18 shows the end-to-end flow for working in Azure Data Explorer and shows how it integrates with other services.

As a practical use case, imagine you're overseeing the operations of a global e-commerce platform. Every click, purchase, and user interaction on your platform generates data. With Azure Data Explorer, you can ingest this data in real time. Using KQL, you can then run complex queries to gauge user behavior, analyze purchase patterns, identify potential website hiccups, and more, all in real time. By using this data-driven approach, you can make instantaneous decisions, be they related to marketing strategies or website optimization.

Azure Data Explorer stands as a formidable tool in the data analytics space, empowering users to make the most of their data. Whether you're a seasoned data analyst or just starting, ADX offers a blend of power and flexibility that can transform the way you view and utilize data.

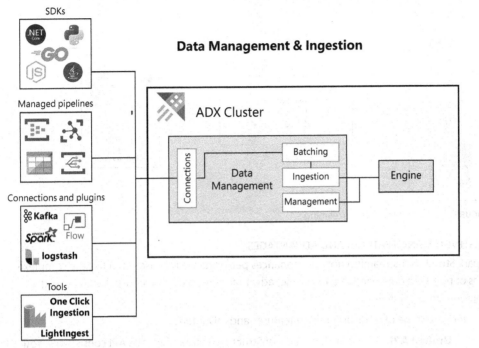

FIGURE 4-18 Azure Data Explorer

Spark Structured Streaming

In today's fast-paced digital landscape, staying ahead often requires having the right tools to process and analyze streaming data seamlessly. While there are numerous technologies at the forefront of this revolution, Apache Spark's Structured Streaming stands out as an exceptional choice. This section will guide you through its intricacies, helping you grasp its underpinnings and recognize how it can be a game-changer in your real-time analytics endeavors.

UNDERSTANDING SPARK STRUCTURED STREAMING

Spark Structured Streaming is a scalable and fault-tolerant stream processing engine built on the Spark platform. It allows you to express your streaming computation the same way you would express a batch computation on static data. This unified approach simplifies the development process and makes switching between batch and stream processing almost effortless. Figure 4-19 illustrates the Spark Structured Streaming workflow.

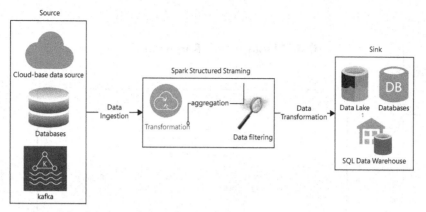

FIGURE 4-19 Spark Structured Streaming

DISTINGUISHING FEATURES AND ADVANTAGES

Spark Structured Streaming not only enhances performance but also simplifies the complexities of real-time data handling. Its distinct advantages lie in its ease of use, accuracy, and integration capabilities.

Here are some of its distinguishing features and advantages:

- **Unified API:** One of the hallmarks of Structured Streaming is its API consistency. You can use the same dataset/dataframe API for both batch and streaming data, making your codebase more streamlined and maintainable.

- **Event-time processing:** It supports window-based operations, allowing you to group records by event-time windows, which is particularly useful when dealing with out-of-order data or when processing data generated in different time zones.

- **Fault tolerance:** With built-in checkpointing and state management, Spark ensures data integrity and allows for seamless recovery from failures.

- **Integration with popular data sources and sinks:** Structured Streaming supports a vast array of sources (such as Kafka, Flume, and Kinesis) and sinks (such as databases, dashboards, and even file systems), providing immense flexibility in how you handle your data streams.

For example, imagine managing a vast transportation network with hundreds of sensors on roads, bridges, and tunnels. These sensors emit data every second, capturing traffic volumes, vehicle speeds, and even environmental conditions. With Spark Structured Streaming, you can ingest this real-time data and process it to gain insights instantly. For instance, analyzing traffic patterns in real time can help pre-empt congestion, making proactive traffic management decisions possible. Similarly, the rapid analysis of environmental data can warn about adverse conditions, allowing for timely interventions.

Spark Structured Streaming, with its powerful capabilities, sets the standard for real-time data processing. Whether your use case revolves around real-time analytics, monitoring, or any scenario that requires instantaneous insights from streaming data, Structured Streaming stands ready to deliver.

Skill 4.3 Describe data visualization in Microsoft Power BI

Dive into the transformative world of data visualization with Microsoft Power BI, a tool that not only brings your data to life but also empowers you to extract insights with unparalleled ease and finesse. As you delve deeper into this segment, imagine the vast swathes of data, currently sitting in spreadsheets or databases and metamorphosing into vibrant charts, intricate graphs, and interactive dashboards. With Power BI, you can tailor every detail of your visualizations to your precise needs.

Picture a dashboard where sales metrics, customer demographics, and operational efficiencies merge seamlessly, with each visual element telling its part of the larger story, as shown in Figure 4-20. That's the promise of Power BI, a canvas where data finds its voice. And while the visual elements captivate, remember that beneath them lie robust analytical capabilities. Want to drill down into a specific data point? Curious about trends over time? Power BI is more than up to the task, offering you both the broad view and the minute details.

In this section, you'll encounter vivid examples that underscore the versatility and power of Power BI. From crafting simple bar charts to designing multidimensional maps, you'll learn the art and science of making data dance to your tune.

And while our guidance here is comprehensive, Power BI's expansive capabilities mean there's always more to explore. Consider referring to Microsoft's official resources for deeper dives, advanced tutorials, and community-driven insights. Let's embark on this enlightening journey, ensuring that, by its end, you're not just a data analyst but also a data storyteller.

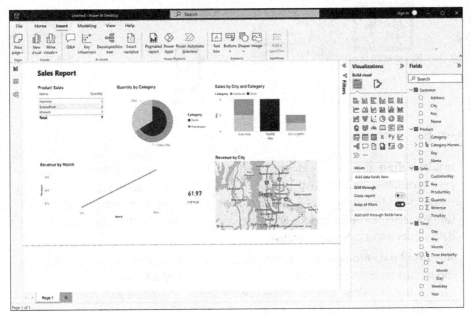

FIGURE 4-20 Power BI interactive dashboard

This skill covers how to:
- Identify capabilities of Power BI
- Describe features of data models in Power BI
- Identify appropriate visualization for data

Identify capabilities of Power BI

When you dive into Power BI, you're immersing yourself in a universe of functionalities, each tailored to elevate your data visualization and analytical skills. Here's a guide to help you navigate and harness the essential capabilities of this remarkable tool.

- **Seamless data integration:** At the heart of every great visualization lies the data that drives it. With Power BI you can connect effortlessly to a diverse range of data sources, be it local databases, cloud-based solutions, Excel spreadsheets, or third-party platforms, as shown in Figure 4-21. The beauty of it is that once the data is connected, you can consolidate and transform that data, paving the way for rich, meaningful visualizations.

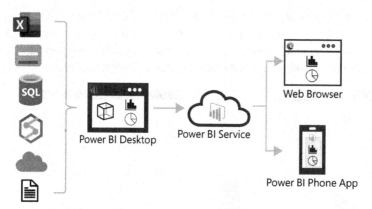

FIGURE 4-21 Power BI data ingestion process

- **Intuitive drag-and-drop features:** You don't need to be a coding wizard to craft compelling visuals in Power BI. With its user-friendly interface, designing everything from simple charts to complex dashboards becomes an intuitive, drag-and-drop affair. Picture yourself effortlessly juxtaposing a line graph next to a pie chart, bringing multiple data stories into a coherent narrative.

- **Advanced data modeling:** Beyond its visualization prowess, Power BI arms you with robust data modeling tools. With features like Data Analysis Expressions (DAX), you can create custom calculations, derive new measures, and model your data in ways that resonate best with your analysis needs.

- **Interactive reports and dashboards:** Static visuals tell only half the story. With Power BI, your visualizations come alive, offering interactive capabilities that encourage exploration. Imagine a sales dashboard where clicking a region dynamically updates all associated charts, revealing granular insights with a mere click.

- **Collaboration and sharing:** Crafting the perfect visualization is one thing; sharing it is another. Power BI streamlines collaboration, meaning you can publish reports, share dashboards, and even embed visuals into apps or websites. Your insights, once confined to your device, can now reach a global audience or targeted stakeholders with ease.

As a practical example, consider you're managing the sales division for a global enterprise. With Power BI, you can effortlessly integrate sales data from various regions, model it to account for currency differences, and craft a dynamic dashboard. Now, with a simple click, stakeholders can dive into regional sales, identify top-performing products, and even forecast future trends.

As your proficiency with Power BI grows, there's always more to discover. As you chart your data journey with Power BI, remember that every insight you unearth has the potential to inform, inspire, and innovate.

> **NEED MORE REVIEW?**   **POWER BI CAPABILITIES**
>
> You can learn more about Power BI capabilities at *learn.microsoft.com/en-us/training/modules/explore-fundamentals-data-visualization/2-power-bi.*

Describe features of data models in Power BI

When you work with Power BI, you're not just interacting with visual representations of data; you're engaging with a meticulously structured data model. The depth and breadth of this model dictate the stories you can extract from your data. This section is a more detailed guide to the intricate features of data models in Power BI and how they set the stage for data-driven narratives.

Relationships

At the heart of your data model are relationships. They let you connect different tables for richer, multidimensional analysis. Think of relationships as bridging islands of data so they can talk to each other. For instance, as shown in Figure 4-22, you can link a Sales table to a Products table to reveal insights about which products drive the most revenue.

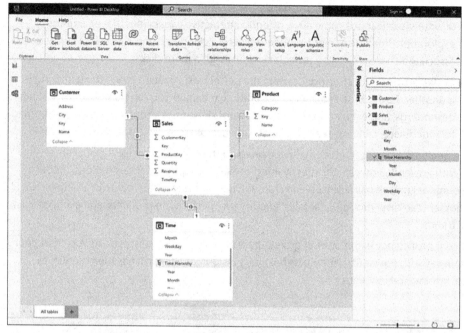

FIGURE 4-22 Power BI table (entity) relationship

BASICS OF TABLE RELATIONSHIPS

In the world of data modeling, especially within tools like Power BI, understanding the basics of table relationships is akin to learning the grammar of a language. These relationships are fundamental to how you interpret and interact with your data. Central to these relationships are concepts like keys and their types, the nature of the connections between tables, and the impact of these connections on data filtering and analysis. Here's a closer look at these foundational elements:

- **Primary and foreign keys:** At the heart of any table relationship is the concept of keys. A primary key is a unique identifier for a record in a table. In contrast, a foreign key in one table points to the primary key in another table, establishing a link between them. It's this connection that facilitates data retrieval across multiple tables.

- **One-to-many and many-to-one relationships:** These are the most common types of relationships you'll encounter. In a one-to-many relationship, a single record in the first table can relate to multiple records in the second table, but not vice versa. Conversely, in many-to-one relationships, multiple records from the first table correspond to a single record in the second table.

- **Many-to-many relationships:** Occasionally, you might find that multiple records in one table relate to multiple records in another table. This complex relationship type, known as many-to-many, was historically handled using bridge tables, but Power BI now offers native support, simplifying its implementation.

- **Cross-filtering and direction:** Relationships in Power BI have a direction, dictating how filters are applied across related tables. This directionality ensures that when you apply a filter to one table, related tables are automatically filtered, preserving data context and integrity.

EXPLORING SCHEMAS

These are the different types of schemas:

- **Star schema:** One of the most prevalent schema designs in Power BI, the star schema consists of a central fact table surrounded by dimension tables. The fact table houses quantitative data (like sales amounts), while dimension tables contain descriptive attributes (like product names or customer details). This structure, resembling a star as shown in Figure 4-23, ensures streamlined data queries and optimal performance.

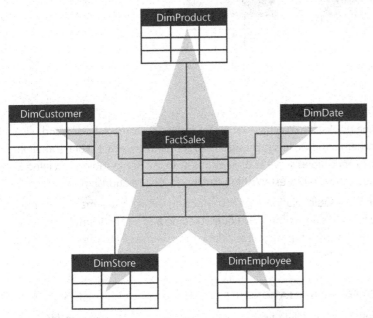

FIGURE 4-23 Star schema

- **Snowflake schema:** An evolution of the star schema, the snowflake schema sees dimension tables normalized into additional tables, as shown in Figure 4-24. This schema can be more complex but offers a more granulated approach to data relationships, making it apt for intricate datasets.

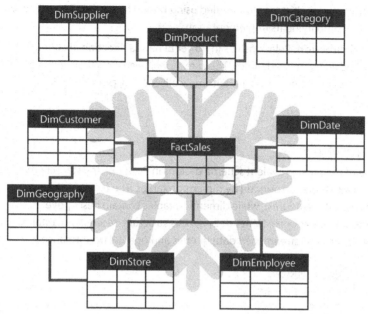

FIGURE 4-24 Snowflake schema

A PRACTICAL SCENARIO

Imagine running an online bookstore. You have tables for orders, customers, books, and authors. Using the star schema, the Orders table sits at the center as your fact table, containing transaction amounts. The other tables serve as dimensions, with the Books table containing a foreign key linking to the Authors table, establishing a many-to-one relationship.

Harnessing the potential of table relationships and choosing the right schema in Power BI isn't just a technical endeavor; it's an art form. By understanding and correctly implementing these relationships, you're crafting a tapestry where data flows seamlessly to offer insights that are both deep and interconnected.

> **NEED MORE REVIEW?   POWER BI RELATIONSHIPS**
>
> You can learn more about Power BI relationships at *learn.microsoft.com/en-us/power-bi/transform-model/desktop-relationship-view*.

Hierarchies

Hierarchies in Power BI allow you to layer different fields in a structured order, offering a multilevel perspective on your data. At a basic level, think of hierarchies as ladders of information, where each rung offers a more granular view than the last.

For instance, in a time hierarchy, you might start with years and descend to months, then weeks, and, finally, days. Each level represents a deeper dive into your data, allowing for detailed drill-down analysis. As shown in Figure 4-25, you are able to view your total yearly sales and then drill down to see a more detailed breakdown of your yearly sales by month.

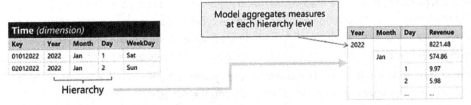

FIGURE 4-25 Power BI hierarchies

WHY HIERARCHIES MATTER

In the realm of data analytics within Power BI, hierarchies represent a fundamental and sophisticated mechanism for organizing and dissecting complex datasets. These structured frameworks are not merely for organizational clarity; they serve as critical tools for enhancing analytical depth and navigational efficiency. Hierarchies in Power BI facilitate a multilayered approach to data examination, providing a powerful means to dissect, understand, and visualize data in a methodical and meaningful way. The following are some essential facets of hierarchies that underscore their significance in professional and technical data analysis:

- **Efficient data exploration:** With hierarchies, you can seamlessly navigate between different levels of data. This efficiency facilitates intuitive data exploration, letting you zoom in on details or pull back to view broader trends.

- **Enhanced visualizations:** Hierarchies bring a dynamic dimension to visualizations. Whether it's a column chart or a map, the ability to drill down through hierarchical levels enriches the visual story, making it more interactive and engaging.

- **Consistent analysis framework:** Hierarchies provide a structured framework for analysis. By establishing a clear order of fields, they ensure consistency in how data is viewed and analyzed across reports and dashboards.

CONSTRUCTING HIERARCHIES

Creating a hierarchy in Power BI is straightforward. In the Fields pane, you can simply drag one field onto another to initiate a hierarchy. From there, you can add or rearrange fields, tailoring the hierarchy to your analytical needs.

A PRACTICAL ILLUSTRATION

Imagine managing a retail chain with stores across multiple countries. You could construct a geographical hierarchy with the following levels:

Continent (e.g., North America)

Country (e.g., United States)

State (e.g., California)

City (e.g., San Francisco)

Store Location (e.g., Market Street)

With this hierarchy in place, a map visualization in Power BI becomes a dynamic exploration tool. At the highest level, you see sales by continent. As you drill down, you traverse through countries, states, and cities, finally landing on individual store locations. This hierarchical journey offers insights ranging from global sales trends down to the performance of a single store.

In the realm of Power BI, hierarchies are more than just structural tools; they're gateways to layered insights. By understanding and adeptly utilizing them, you can craft data stories that resonate with depth, clarity, and context.

> ***NEED MORE REVIEW?*** **POWER BI HIERARCHIES**
>
> You can learn more about Power BI hierarchies at *learn.microsoft.com/en-us/analysis-services/ tabular-models/hierarchies-ssas-tabular?view=asallproducts-allversions*.

Measures and Calculated Columns

Data seldom fits perfectly into our analytical narratives. Often, it requires tweaking, transformation, or entirely new computations to reveal the insights we seek. Power BI acknowledges this need with two potent features: measures and calculated columns. These tools, driven by the powerful DAX language, grant you the capability to sculpt and refine your data. Here, we'll dive deep into these features, elucidating their distinctions and utilities and bringing them to life with hands-on examples.

A *measure* is a calculation applied to a dataset, usually an aggregation like sum, average, or count, that dynamically updates based on the context in which it's used. For instance, the same measure can provide the total sales for an entire year, a specific month, or even a single product, depending on the visualization or filter context. Measures are immensely useful when you want to examine aggregated data. They respond to user interactions, ensuring that as filters or slicers are applied to a report, the measures reflect the appropriate, contextual data.

A *calculated column* is a custom column added to an existing table in your data model. The values of this column are computed during data load and are based on a DAX formula that uses existing columns. When you need a new column that's derived from existing data—for computations or classifications—a calculated column is the go-to tool. Unlike measures, these values remain static and are calculated row by row.

Measures are for aggregating and are context-aware, while calculated columns add new, static data to your tables.

As an example, imagine you're analyzing sales data for a chain of bookstores. You might create a measure named Total Sales using the formula Total Sales = SUM(Transactions[SalesAmount]). This measure can display total sales across all stores but will adjust to show sales for a specific store if you filter by one.

Using the same bookstore data, suppose you want to classify books into price categories: Budget, Mid-Range, and Premium. You can create a calculated column named Price Category with a formula like this:

```
Price Category =
IF(Books[Price] < 10, "Budget",
IF(Books[Price] <= 30, "Mid-Range", "Premium"))
```

This adds a new Price Category column to your Books table, classifying each book based on its price.

Harnessing measures and calculated columns in Power BI are akin to being handed a chisel as you sculpt a statue from a block of marble. They allow you to shape, refine, and perfect your data, ensuring your analyses and visualizations are both precise and insightful. To delve deeper into the world of DAX and custom calculations, the official Microsoft documentation provides a treasure trove of knowledge, from foundational concepts to advanced techniques.

> **NEED MORE REVIEW? DAX AND CUSTOM CALCULATIONS**
>
> You can learn more about DAX and custom calculations at *learn.microsoft.com/en-us/ power-bi/transform-model/desktop-quickstart-learn-dax-basics.*

Data categorization

Data categorization in Power BI involves assigning a specific type or category to a data column, thereby providing hints to Power BI about the nature of the data. This categorization ensures that Power BI understands and appropriately represents the data, especially when used in visuals or calculations.

WHY DATA CATEGORIZATION MATTERS

Data categorization in Power BI is pivotal for extracting maximum value from your datasets, impacting everything from visualization choices to data integrity. It enables Power BI to provide tailored visual suggestions, enhances the effectiveness of natural language queries, and serves as a critical tool for data validation. Here's why categorizing your data correctly matters:

- **Enhanced visualization interpretation:** By understanding the context of your data, Power BI can auto-suggest relevant visuals. Geographical data, for instance, would prompt map-based visualizations, while date fields might suggest time-series charts.

- **Improved search and Q&A features:** Power BI's Q&A tool, which allows natural language queries, leans on data categorization. When you ask for "sales by city," the tool knows to reference geographical data due to the categorization of the City column.

- **Data validation:** Categorization can act as a form of data validation. By marking a column as a date, any nondate values become evident, highlighting potential data quality issues.

COMMON DATA TYPES IN POWER BI

In Power BI, the clarity and accuracy of your reports hinge on understanding the core data types at your disposal. Each data type serves a specific purpose, shaping how information is stored, analyzed, and presented. The following are common data types:

- **Text:** Generic textual data, from product names to descriptions
- **Whole number:** Numeric data without decimal points, like quantities or counts
- **Decimal number:** Numeric data with decimal precision, suitable for price or rate data
- **Date/time:** Fields that have timestamps, including date, time, or both

COMMON DATA CATEGORIES IN POWER BI

In Power BI, data categorization plays a crucial role in tailoring visualizations and enhancing report interactivity. Here is a list of common data categories found in Power BI:

- **Geographical:** Includes various subcategories such as Address, City, Country, Latitude, Longitude, Postal Code, etc., facilitating map-based visualizations
- **Web URL:** Web addresses, hyperlinks within Power BI reports

A PRACTICAL ILLUSTRATION

Suppose you're working with a dataset that captures details of art galleries worldwide. The dataset includes the gallery name, city, country, average visitor count, website, and date of establishment.

- "Gallery Name" would be categorized as Text.
- "City" and "Country" fall under the Geographical category.
- "Average Visitor Count" is a Whole Number.
- "Website" is categorized as a Web URL.
- "Date of Establishment" is assigned the Date/Time category.

With these categorizations in place, Power BI can effortlessly visualize a map pinpointing gallery location worldwide or create a time-series chart showcasing the growth of galleries over the years.

Understanding and effectively leveraging data categorization in Power BI transform your data from raw numbers and text into a coherent story, adding layers of context, meaning, and depth.

> **NEED MORE REVIEW?** **DATA CATEGORIZATION AND DATA TYPES**
>
> You can learn more about data categorization and data types at *learn.microsoft.com/en-us/ power-bi/transform-model/desktop-data-categorization* and *learn.microsoft.com/en-us/ power-bi/connect-data/desktop-data-types*.

Quick Measures

In the vast and intricate world of data analysis, time is of the essence. Power BI recognizes this, and in its arsenal of features aimed at streamlining your analytical journey, you'll find Quick Measures, a tool designed to expedite the process of creating complex calculations. It's about making what was once convoluted accessible and swift. Dive into this section to discover the features of Quick Measures and how you can leverage them effectively.

Quick Measures is a compilation of prebuilt DAX formulas in Power BI that automate commonly used calculations. Instead of manually writing out a DAX expression for a particular metric, you can use Quick Measures to generate these formulas for you, based on your data model and your selected fields.

THE POWER OF QUICK MEASURES

Quick Measures in Power BI streamlines the analytical process by offering a suite of predefined calculations. Here is a list of the key benefits Quick Measures brings to Power BI:

- **Efficiency:** You no longer need to remember or construct intricate DAX formulas for common calculations. Quick Measures offers a library of these, ready to be deployed.
- **Consistency:** By using standardized formulas, you ensure consistency in your metrics, which is especially beneficial if sharing reports or datasets across teams.
- **Learning tool:** For those new to DAX or Power BI, Quick Measures can act as an educational tool, offering insights into how specific formulas are constructed.

POPULAR QUICK MEASURES

Power BI's Quick Measures feature offers a range of popular calculations designed to enhance data analysis. The following are the key measures:

- **Time intelligence:** Gathering year-to-date, quarter-to-date, month-over-month changes, and running totals
- **Mathematical operations:** Calculating percentages, differences, or products of columns
- **Statistical measures:** Calculating averages, medians, or standard deviations
- **Aggregations:** Summing, counting, or finding the minimum or maximum of a column based on certain conditions

A PRACTICAL WALK-THROUGH

Imagine you're analyzing sales data and you want to understand month-over-month growth for a particular product.

Instead of manually creating a DAX formula to compute this, follow these steps:

1. In a table or matrix visual, right-click a numerical column, like Sales, and select "New quick measure," as shown in Figure 4-26.

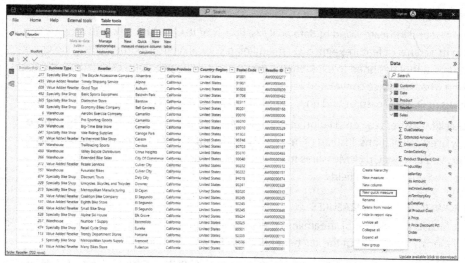

FIGURE 4-26 "New quick measure" menu item

2. From the Quick Measures dialog box, choose "Month-over-month change" from the Time Intelligence category.

3. Follow the prompts, selecting the appropriate fields (e.g., Sales and Date).

4. Once added, the new quick measure will compute the month-over-month growth for sales, dynamically adjusting based on filters or slicers applied to your report.

By employing Quick Measures, you've saved precious time and ensured accuracy, letting Power BI handle the complexities of DAX on your behalf.

When embarking on the Power BI journey, you'll find many tools designed to make your analytical process smoother and more efficient. Quick Measures stands as a testament to this, offering you a shortcut to insights without compromising on depth or accuracy.

> **NEED MORE REVIEW?** **QUICK MEASURES**
>
> You can learn more about Quick Measures at *learn.microsoft.com/en-us/power-bi/ transform-model/desktop-quick-measures#quick-measure-example.*

EXAM TIP

Remember, your knowledge is your strength, but understanding the context in which to apply that knowledge is key to success on the exam:

- Large-scale analytics
  - Don't just memorize what services Azure offers; be aware of when and why you'd use them in different scenarios.
  - Familiarize yourself with the specifics of data ingestion in Azure. Terms like *data lakes and data factories* should be second nature.

- Real-time data analytics
  - Differentiate clearly between batch and streaming data; the handling and tools for each differ significantly.
  - Recognize the use cases for real-time analytics, from financial transactions to social media monitoring.
- Visualization with Power BI
  - Dive deep into Power BI's features. Knowing how to model data within it can be crucial.
  - Visualization is more than aesthetics. Understand the importance of data structure, categorization, and representation in Power BI.
- Azure Services for data warehousing
  - Azure Synapse Analytics isn't just another data warehouse; remember its integrative capabilities with AI and Power BI.
  - Azure Databricks, HDInsight, and Data Factory have overlapping functionalities but distinct strengths. Know the distinguishing factors.
- General tip
  - Context is king. When given a scenario in the exam, pay attention to the business needs and constraints; they'll guide your answer.

Chapter summary

This summary encapsulates the main topics of this chapter, providing a clear overview of its content and structure:

- Large-scale analytics
  - **Managing vast volumes of data:** Crucial for ensuring comprehensive analysis and informed decision-making
  - **Data ingestion and processing:** Streamlining data flows and preprocessing
  - **Analytical data stores:** Ensuring efficient, scalable, and fast data retrieval
  - **Azure's answer to data warehousing:** Synapse Analytics and its scalable architecture
- Real-time data analytics
  - **Distinguishing between batch and streaming data:** Clarifies the approach for processing diverse data types in real-time and batch scenarios
  - **Need for real-time analytics:** Timely insights and immediate action
  - **Azure's offerings:** Stream Analytics, Databricks, and HDInsight
- Visualization with Power BI
  - **Power BI transforms complex data into comprehensible visuals:** Enhances data interpretation and decision-making processes.

- **In-depth look at Power BI's capabilities:** From dashboards to drill-down reports
- **The data model in Power BI:** Structuring data for effective visualization
- **Power of data visualization:** Turning raw numbers into actionable insights
- Azure services for data warehousing
  - **Azure Synapse Analytics:** The next-gen data warehouse
  - **Azure Databricks:** Blending big data and AI
  - **Azure HDInsight:** Harnessing the power of open-source analytics frameworks
  - **Azure Data Factory:** The linchpin in Azure's data integration services

Thought experiment

You're a data engineer at TechNova, a multinational corporation. TechNova is venturing into a new analytics project, aiming to collect data from various global branches, seeking real-time analytics capabilities, and hoping to visualize the data for senior stakeholders. The company has chosen Azure as its cloud platform. Your role is to identify and recommend the optimal Azure services for each stage of the data journey.

1. As you're charting the journey from raw data capture to insightful visualizations, which sequence of Azure services would best suit this flow?

   A. Azure Data Factory → Azure Data Sources → Power BI → Azure Synapse Analytics → Azure Analysis Services

   B. Azure Data Sources → Azure Synapse Analytics → Azure Data Factory → Azure Analysis Services → Power BI

   C. Azure Data Sources → Azure Data Factory → Azure Synapse Analytics → Azure Analysis Services → Power BI

   D. Power BI → Azure Data Factory → Azure Synapse Analytics → Azure Data Sources → Azure Analysis Services

2. For real-time analytics, you're debating between batch and streaming data. If immediate data processing is a priority, which method do you think is best?

   A. Batch data

   B. Streaming data

   C. Azure Analysis Services

   D. Azure Data Factory

3. To foster a data-driven culture, business users must interpret data without constant IT intervention. Which Azure service would you select to make raw data more intuitive for them?

   A. Power BI

   B. Azure Synapse Analytics

C. Azure Data Lake

D. Azure Analysis Services

4. The leadership team desires a tool to unearth and explore insights from complex datasets. Which tool would you introduce for dynamic and comprehensive visual exploration?

A. Azure Portal

B. Power BI

C. Azure Synapse Analytics

D. Azure Monitor

5. While considering scalability in large-scale analytics, which Azure service would you pick to ensure a scalable data warehousing solution?

A. Azure Blob Storage

B. Power BI

C. Azure Synapse Analytics

D. Azure Analysis Services

6. You want to run large-scale data processing tasks using popular open-source frameworks. Which Azure service aligns with this requirement?

A. Azure Data Factory

B. Azure Databricks

C. Azure Logic Apps

D. Azure Blob Storage

7. You're keen on exploring a fully managed cloud service that provides real-time analytics from streaming data. Where would you look?

A. Azure Analysis Services

B. Azure HDInsight

C. Azure Stream Analytics

D. Azure Data Lake

8. To stitch together a range of data-driven services into orchestrated workflows, which Azure service would you harness?

A. Azure Stream Analytics

B. Power BI

C. Azure Synapse Analytics

D. Azure Data Factory

9. You've been asked to deploy a tool that allows for batch, interactive, and real-time analytics, harnessing the best of open-source technologies. What would your pick be?

A. Azure Databricks

B. Azure Data Factory

C. Power BI

D. Azure Logic Apps

10. If data visualization with deep integration into other Azure services is what you're after, which tool would you gravitate toward?

A. Azure Stream Analytics

B. Power BI

C. Azure Synapse Analytics

D. Azure Data Lake

11. If you need a service to store large volumes of structured and unstructured data, facilitating batch and real-time analytics, which Azure service fits the bill?

A. Azure Blob Storage

B. Azure Data Factory

C. Azure Synapse Analytics

D. Azure Data Lake

12. You're considering a NoSQL database solution on Azure that offers multimodel capabilities. Which service would you choose?

A. Azure SQL Database

B. Azure Synapse Analytics

C. Azure Cosmos DB

D. Azure Blob Storage

13. If you're after an Apache Hadoop–based service that integrates with popular open-source frameworks, which Azure service would you zero in on?

A. Azure Databricks

B. Azure Stream Analytics

C. Azure Data Factory

D. Azure HDInsight

14. For a reliable event streaming platform that can process millions of events per second, which Azure service would you bank on?

A. Azure Stream Analytics

B. Azure Cosmos DB

C. Azure Synapse Analytics

D. Azure Kafka

15. If you're gearing up for a comprehensive analytics service that integrates with various machine learning tools and provides native integration with Power BI, which Azure tool would be your top choice?

A. Azure Stream Analytics

B. Power BI

C. Azure Synapse Analytics

D. Azure Data Lake

Thought experiment answers

Each of these questions, along with their explanations, is designed to fortify your understanding of Azure's offerings and how they interact in a real-world setting.

1. **C** Azure data sources → Azure Data Factory → Azure Synapse Analytics → Azure Analysis Services → Power BI

   Explanation: The data journey starts with the Azure data sources, capturing the raw, unprocessed data. Azure Data Factory then steps in, orchestrating and moving this data to ensure it's in the right place and format. Azure Synapse Analytics offers large-scale data processing capabilities to do in-depth analyses and merge diverse datasets. After this processing, Azure Analysis Services refines this data even further. By laying a semantic layer over it, business users find it more interpretable. Finally, Power BI is the visualization maestro, converting this well-processed data into interactive and informative visual insights.

2. **B** Streaming data

   Explanation: Streaming data is like the live broadcast of data landscapes. Unlike its counterpart, batch data, which operates more like a scheduled TV show, streaming data is continuous. In situations where immediacy is crucial (think monitoring live transactions or tracking system health in real time), streaming data shines. It allows for instantaneous data capture, processing, and reaction, granting you the advantage of time-sensitive insights.

3. **D** Azure Analysis Services

   Explanation: Azure Analysis Services is akin to a skilled interpreter. In a world where data language can be intricate and hard to decipher, Analysis Services steps in, breaking down the complexity. By overlaying a semantic model onto the raw data, it makes this data speak the language of the business. It translates complex structures and relationships into formats and terminologies that are more familiar to business users. This not only encourages self-service analytics but also fosters a deeper trust in data-driven decision-making.

4. **B** Power BI

   Explanation: Power BI isn't just a visualization tool; it's a data exploration powerhouse. Imagine having a magnifying glass that not only zooms into data but also paints it in vibrant, comprehensible colors. Power BI offers dashboards and visuals that are not just static images but interactive canvases. Whether it's drilling down into specific data points, changing data views on the fly, or asking natural language questions, Power BI facilitates a deeper, more interactive engagement with data. It empowers users, even those not technically inclined, to seek answers, spot patterns, and make informed decisions.

5.   **C** Azure Synapse Analytics

Explanation: Azure Synapse Analytics is your go-to for a data warehousing solution that not only scales but does so without causing a dent in performance. Unlike traditional systems where scaling up often meant extended downtimes or complex processes, Synapse Analytics provides on-demand scalability. Whether you're dealing with a sudden influx of data or foreseeing increased query loads, Synapse lets you upscale or downscale with ease, ensuring cost-efficiency and performance optimization.

6.   **B** Azure Databricks

Explanation: Azure Databricks offers a seamless integration of Databricks with Azure, providing an environment tailor-made for large-scale data processing tasks using frameworks like Apache Spark. It's not just about processing power; it's also about collaboration. Databricks ensures data engineers, data scientists, and business analysts can work together, fostering innovation and efficiency.

7.   **C** Azure Stream Analytics

Explanation: Azure Stream Analytics is your lens into the real-time world of data. With the ability to ingest, process, and output streaming data to any Azure service, Stream Analytics lets you react promptly to emerging patterns and anomalies. From monitoring IoT device outputs to live telemetry, it gives you real-time insights that can be pivotal in decision-making.

8.   **D** Azure Data Factory

Explanation: When it comes to orchestrating and automating data-driven workflows, Azure Data Factory stands out. Think of it as the maestro in an orchestra, ensuring each instrument (or service) plays its part at the right time. With Data Factory, you can create, schedule, and manage data integration services that wrangle and move data between different supported endpoints.

9.   **A** Azure Databricks

Explanation: Azure Databricks is a testament to the power of collaborative open-source frameworks. Leveraging Apache Spark's capabilities, Databricks facilitates batch, interactive, and real-time analytics, making it a versatile platform for diverse data tasks. Its collaborative workspace fosters teamwork, bridging the gap between data engineers and data scientists.

10.   **B** Power BI

Explanation: While several Azure services offer aspects of data visualization, Power BI is a leader in this realm. Its deep integration with other Azure services ensures a seamless data journey from source to visualization. The tool's dashboards and reports are not just visually appealing but are interactive, offering drill-down capabilities and rich insights.

11. **D** Azure Data Lake

    Explanation: Azure Data Lake is designed with massive data volumes in mind. Catering to both structured and unstructured data, it's versatile. It's not just a storage solution; its analytical capabilities ensure you can run diverse analytics, be it batch or real time, directly on the stored data. The service embodies the essence of "store once, analyze many" paradigms.

12. **C** Azure Cosmos DB

    Explanation: When it comes to NoSQL offerings on Azure with multimodel capabilities, Azure Cosmos DB emerges as a clear winner. With its globally distributed architecture, it offers multimodel database services for large-scale applications. Be it document, key-value, graph, or columnar data models, Cosmos DB accommodates them, providing scalability, resilience, and a performance guarantee.

13. **D** Azure HDInsight

    Explanation: Azure HDInsight is Azure's offering for those who are keen on harnessing the capabilities of Apache Hadoop in a cloud environment. Not just limited to Hadoop, HDInsight supports a plethora of open-source frameworks such as Spark, Hive, LLAP, Kafka, and more, making it a potent solution for diverse big data tasks.

14. **D** Azure Kafka

    Explanation: Azure offers Kafka as a part of the Azure HDInsight service. Renowned for its capabilities as an event streaming platform, Kafka on Azure can handle millions of events per second. Whether you're ingesting data from websites, applications, or IoT devices, Kafka ensures real-time processing and analytics, making it pivotal for time-sensitive insights.

15. **C** Azure Synapse Analytics

    Explanation: Azure Synapse Analytics is a testament to the evolution of data warehousing solutions. Beyond just warehousing, Synapse integrates seamlessly with various machine learning tools, allowing for advanced analytics. Its native Power BI integration ensures that the insights gleaned are readily visualized, making the transition from data to decision smoother and more informed.

Scenario Exercises

ZenithTech is a leading tech retailer with a robust online presence. They've recently decided to expand their reach by launching physical stores across the country. This expansion requires them to integrate in-store purchase data with their existing online transaction database. They've turned to Azure's suite of analytics tools to help them with this.

Before you start, you'll need an Azure subscription (*azure.microsoft.com/en-us/free/*) in which you have administrative-level access.

Task 1: Large-scale data ingestion and processing

1. Set up Azure Data Factory.

    A. Open the Azure portal and search for Data Factory.

    B. Click Add and fill in the subscription details, resource group, region, and name for the Data Factory instance.

    C. Review other configurations and click "Review + create."

2. Ingest data to Azure Data Lake Storage.

    A. Once your data factory is deployed, go to Author.

    B. Under datasets, click + to create a new dataset.

    C. Choose your data source (e.g., SQL database for in-store data) and provide connection details.

    D. Create an output dataset and select Azure Data Lake Storage.

    E. Map columns from your source to destination.

    F. Under activities, choose "Copy data" and link the input and output datasets.

3. Stream Online Transactions with Azure Stream Analytics.

    A. In the Azure portal, search for "Stream Analytics job."

    B. Fill in job details, including job name, region, and resource group.

    C. Under inputs, add your online transaction source.

    D. For outputs, add the destination as Azure Data Lake or Synapse Analytics.

    E. In the query section, define the data transformation or filtering rules, if any.

Task 2: An analytical data store

1. Set up Azure Synapse analytics.

    A. Search for Azure Synapse in the Azure portal and click Add.

    B. Configure the basics like subscription, resource group, and name.

    C. Navigate to the created Synapse workspace, connect to your Azure Data Lake Storage. Under "Security + networking," configure managed private endpoints.

2. Link data:

    A. Within Synapse Studio, click the Data tab.

    B. Connect to external datasets and add them to Synapse.

    C. Use Data Flow to transform and clean data, if necessary.

Task 3: Real-time analytics

1. Implement Azure Databricks.
   - A. Open the Azure portal and create a new Databricks workspace.
   - B. Launch the workspace and create a cluster by choosing the runtime version.
   - C. Once the cluster is ready, open a new notebook.
   - D. Using Spark SQL or PySpark, write and run analytics queries on your data.
2. Distinguish data types.
   - A. Use timestamp fields in your data.
   - B. In Databricks, filter data within the last X minutes for real time and beyond for historical.
   - C. Visualize the results using Databricks' built-in visuals or connect to Power BI.

Task 4: Power BI visualization

1. Connect Power BI to Azure Synapse.
   - A. Launch Power BI Desktop.
   - B. Under Get Data, find Azure services, and select Azure Synapse Analytics.
   - C. Authenticate and select the tables or views to pull into Power BI.
2. Design a Power BI dashboard:
   - A. In Power BI, use the drag-and-drop functionality to place data fields onto the report canvas.
   - B. Choose appropriate visuals such as bar charts, pie charts, or tables.
   - C. Apply filters, slicers, or drill-downs to make the report interactive.

Task 5: Azure data warehousing services

1. Evaluate Azure HDInsight.
   - A. Review your data volume and variety.
   - B. If you have a large amount of unstructured data or need to run Hadoop/Spark jobs, consider HDInsight.
2. Optimize Azure Data Factory Pipelines.
   - A. In Data Factory, click the Monitor tab.
   - B. Check for failed or slow-running pipelines.
   - C. Adjust the pipeline settings, like frequency or data partitions.

   Reflection: After completing these tasks, jot down the challenges you faced and how you resolved them. Which Azure services seemed most intuitive to you? Which required a steeper learning curve?

CHAPTER 5

DP-900 Microsoft Azure Data Fundamentals Exam Updates

The purpose of this chapter

For Chapters 1–4, the content should remain relevant throughout the life of this edition. But for this chapter, we will update the content over time. Even after you purchase the book, you'll be able to access a PDF file online with the most up-to-date version of this chapter.

Why do we need to update this chapter after the publication of this book? For these reasons:

- To add more technical content to the book before the next edition is published. This updated PDF chapter will include additional technology content.

- To communicate detail about the next version of the exam, to tell you about our publishing plans for that version, and to help you understand what that means to you.

- To provide an accurate mapping of the current exam objectives to the existing chapter content. Though exam objectives evolve and products are renamed, most of the content in this book will remain accurate and relevant. The online chapter will cover the content of any new objectives, as well as provide explanatory notes on how the new objectives map to the current text.

After the initial publication of this book, Microsoft Press will provide supplemental updates as digital downloads for minor exam updates. If an exam has major changes or accumulates enough minor changes, we will then announce a new edition. We will do our best to provide any updates to you free of charge before we release a new edition. However, if the updates are significant enough in between editions, we may release the updates as a low-priced stand-alone e-book.

If we do produce a free updated version of this chapter, you can access it on the book's product page, simply visit *MicrosoftPressStore.com/ERDP9002e/downloads* to view and download the updated material.

About possible exam updates

Microsoft reviews exam content periodically to ensure that it aligns with the technology and job role associated with the exam. This includes, but is not limited to, incorporating functionality and features related to technology changes, changing skills needed for success within a job role, and revisions to product names. Microsoft updates the exam details page to notify candidates when changes occur. If you have registered this book and an update occurs to this chapter, you will be notified by Microsoft Press about the availability of this updated chapter.

Impact on you and your study plan

Microsoft's information helps you plan, but it also means that the exam might change before you pass the current exam. That impacts you, affecting how we deliver this book to you. This chapter gives us a way to communicate in detail about those changes as they occur. But you should keep an eye on other spaces as well.

For those other information sources to watch, bookmark and check these sites for news:

Microsoft Learn: Check the main source for up-to-date information: microsoft.com/learn. Make sure to sign up for automatic notifications at that page.

Microsoft Press: Find information about products, offers, discounts, and free downloads: *microsoftpressstore.com*. Make sure to register your purchased products.

As changes arise, we will update this chapter with more details about the exam and book content. At that point, we will publish an updated version of this chapter, listing our content plans. That detail will likely include the following:

- Content removed, so if you plan to take the new exam version, you can ignore those when studying
- New content planned per new exam topics, so you know what's coming

The remainder of the chapter shows the new content that may change over time.

News and commentary about the exam objective updates

The updates to the DP-900 exam objectives effective February 1, 2024, reveal a few noteworthy changes and refinements compared to the previous version. The following is commentary on each of the updates:

Audience Profile

- **Before & After Update:** The target audience remains consistent. The exam is aimed at candidates new to working with data in the cloud, requiring familiarity with core data concepts and Microsoft Azure data services.

Describe Core Data Concepts (25–30%)

- **Before & After Update:** This section remains largely unchanged, focusing on representing data (structured, semi-structured, unstructured), data storage options, and common data workloads (transactional, analytical). The roles and responsibilities associated with these workloads are also consistently covered.

Identify Considerations for Relational Data on Azure (20–25%)

- **Before & After Update:** Both versions cover relational concepts, including features of relational data, normalization, SQL statements, and common database objects. A notable change is the explicit mention of the "Azure SQL family of products" in the updated objectives, offering a clearer focus on specific Azure services.

Describe Considerations for Working with Non-Relational Data on Azure (15–20%)

- **Before & After Update:** This section remains consistent in both versions, covering Azure storage capabilities (Blob, File, Table storage) and Azure Cosmos DB features. The emphasis on understanding Azure's storage solutions and Cosmos DB's use cases and APIs continues to be a crucial part of this section.

Describe an Analytics Workload on Azure (25–30%)

- **Before Update:** This section previously included details on Azure services for data warehousing, real-time data analytics technologies (Azure Stream Analytics, Azure Synapse Data Explorer, Spark Structured Streaming), and data visualization in Power BI.

- **After Update:** The updated objectives maintain the focus on large-scale analytics, data warehousing, and real-time data analytics but have removed specific mentions of technologies like Azure Stream Analytics, Azure Synapse Data Explorer, and Spark Structured Streaming. Instead, there's a broader reference to "Microsoft cloud services for real-time analytics," suggesting a more general approach. The section on Power BI remains similar, emphasizing its capabilities, data models, and visualization options.

General Observations:

- The updates indicate a shift toward a more generalized and possibly up-to-date overview of Azure services, especially in the analytics workload section.

- The explicit mention of the Azure SQL family of products under relational data shows an emphasis on Azure-specific services.

- Overall, the changes seem to align the exam more closely with current Azure offerings and trends in cloud data management without significantly altering the core content or focus areas of the exam.

These updates suggest a continued emphasis on ensuring that candidates have a well-rounded understanding of Azure's data services, both relational and non-relational, along with a solid grasp of analytical workloads as they pertain to Azure's environment.

Updated technical content

Describe consideration for real-time data analytics: This section has been marked with a "Minor" change.

Objective mapping

This book is based on the topics and technologies covered on the exam but is not structured based on the specific order of topics in the exam objectives. Table 5-1 maps the current version of the exam objectives to the chapter content, allowing you to locate where a specific exam objective item is covered without having to consult the index.

TABLE 5-1 Exam objectives mapped to chapters

Exam objective	Chapter
Describe core data concept	
Describe ways to represent data ■ Describe features of structured data ■ Describe features of semi-structured data ■ Describe features of unstructured data	1
Identify options for data storage ■ Describe common formats for data files ■ Describe types of databases	1
Describe common data workloads ■ Describe features of transactional workloads ■ Describe features of analytical workloads	1
Identify roles and responsibilities for data workloads ■ Describe responsibilities for database administrators ■ Describe responsibilities for data engineers ■ Describe responsibilities for data analysts	1
Identify considerations for relational data on Azure	
Describe relational concepts ■ Identify features of relational data ■ Describe normalization and its uses ■ Identify common structured query language (SQL) statement ■ Identify common database objects	2
Describe relational Azure data services ■ Describe the Azure SQL family of products including Azure SQL Database, Azure SQL ■ Managed Instance, and SQL Server on Azure Virtual Machines ■ Identify Azure database services for open-source database systems	2

Exam objective	Chapter
Describe considerations for working with non-relational data on Azure	
Describe capabilities of Azure storage	3
■ Describe Azure Blob storage	
■ Describe Azure Data Lake Storage Gen2	
■ Describe Azure File storage	
■ Describe Azure Table storage	
Describe capabilities and features of Azure Cosmos DB	3
■ Identify use cases for Azure Cosmos DB	
■ Describe Azure Cosmos DB APIs	
Describe an analytics workload on Azure	
Describe common elements of large-scale analytics	4
■ Describe large-scale data warehousing architecture	
■ Describe considerations for data ingestion and processing	
■ Describe options for analytical data stores	
■ Describe Azure services for data warehousing	
Describe considerations for real-time data analytics	4
■ Describe the difference between batch and streaming data	
■ Identify Microsoft cloud services for real-time analytics	
Describe data visualization in Microsoft Power BI	4
■ Identify capabilities of Power BI	
■ Describe features of data models in Power BI	
■ Identify appropriate visualization for data	

Index

Numerics

E-F

G

H

I-J

K

Plug into learning at

MicrosoftPressStore.com

The Microsoft Press Store by Pearson offers:

- Free U.S. shipping

- Buy an eBook, get three formats – Includes PDF, EPUB, and MOBI to use with your computer, tablet, and mobile devices

- Print & eBook Best Value Packs

- eBook Deal of the Week – Save up to 50% on featured title

- Newsletter – Be the first to hear about new releases, announcements, special offers, and more

- Register your book – Find companion files, errata, and product updates, plus receive a special coupon* to save on your next purchase

 Pearson

Hear about it first.

Since 1984, Microsoft Press has helped IT professionals, developers, and home office users advance their technical skills and knowledge with books and learning resources.

Sign up today to deliver exclusive offers directly to your inbox.

- New products and announcements

- Free sample chapters

- Special promotions and discounts

- ... and more!

MicrosoftPressStore.com/newsletters

 Pearson